Knowledge From the Stars

through
Wesley H. Bateman,
Federation Telepath

Published by
Light Technology Publishing
P.O. Box 1526
Sedona, AZ 86339

ISBN 0-929385-39-X

Printed by
Mission Possible Commercial Printing
a division of Love Light Communication Services
P.O. Box 1526
Sedona, AZ 86339

Contents

Sasquatch 1

The Finding of Flight 19 8

Flight 19 Update 18

The Secret Of The Flying Saucers 19

The Frequency Barrier 27

Vril Energy: The Psychic Charge Force 36

The Universal Life Field: Levels of Perception 43

The Forces Of Light And Darkness 48

Dulce: How Sweet Is It? 54

Extraterrestrials: Now You See Them, Now You Don't 64

I Am Darafina 69

Yesteryear, A Million Times Yesteryear 79

Mental Investigations Of New Dimensions 89

Hooray for Hollywood 98

The Mind Center 105

The Patrax Projects: Part 1 116

The Patrax Projects: Part 2 124

The Patrax Projects: Part 3 130

The Patrax Projects: Part 4 135

Giant Step

Hello to you on this road of life, you appear to be going my way. How hard has it been to walk this far today?

Rest your burden a little while and sit beside me here. Tho a stranger I appear to you, please do not have fear.

The path that you and I must take is very much the same. Wanting to meet you at this time of life, through galaxies of stars I came.

Your world is waking from a deep, deep sleep. Your thoughts are confused and new. Our path is under a rainbow bridge. May I walk with you?

Awake I've been for many a year, I was up before the dawn. I saw your world go to sleep and watched its awakening yawn.

The rainbow bridge lies just ahead, where your rockets soar through the sky. Beyond that bridge are men like you and a man from there am I.

Rockets are not my way, but a silver disc of light. It matters not of such things, for we're equal in God's sight.

Let us please go hand in hand across God's starry road. Place your burden in my silver disc, it will carry your load.

Step by step we will go on a journey far beyond Mars. Let us take these steps together, they'll be giant steps into the stars.

Wes Bateman

1.

Sasquatch

May 1991

Sasquatch, Yeti, Swamp Ape, and Skunk Ape are several names that have been attached to the elusive giant hairy creatures that are from time to time spotted in the northwest part of the United States, the Himalaya mountains of Nepal, India, and the swamps of Florida and Louisiana. The Indians of the Northwest have legends of these creatures, which most tribes describe as "those that leave large tracks." Thus they are called "Bigfoot" in English.

Plaster casts of footprints supposedly made by these creatures are numerous. Some of this so-called evidence has proved to have been fabricated by individuals wearing large artificial feet over their own. Serious researchers are adept at separating most phony footprints from those they feel are authentic by the distance between tracks and by their depth; the tracks would have to match the stride of a 7- to 8-foot creature and of a depth appropriate to the creature's estimated weight of 550 to 800 pounds.

Most plaster casts thought to be authentic do have one thing in common: No matter what size the foot, the second toe is always reportedly longer than the big toe, whereas in most humans and apes the big toe is the longest.

Stories of sightings and encounters of these creatures have been passed down for ages and still reach us in print by way of supermarket tabloids. Other than the reports which state that the encountered creatures smelled bad and made frightening noises, there is little evidence that they are hostile unless physically threatened.

The Sherpas of Nepal relate that the Yeti, their version of Bigfoot, have stolen some of their women for the purpose of mating. If these stories are true, we must first consider the fact that one species does not have natural desires to mate with another; and secondly, that the creatures' actions in these cases may be based on the fact that they are themselves a form of human.

In the late 1960s a couple returning to their northern California mountain cabin found it in shambles. Canned goods were squashed to the point where they were actually burst open. It was obvious that the contents of the cans were eaten by something with a large appetite. Spilled flour provided the medium for giant footprints that seemed to go from place to place, stopping at things that might have been of curiosity, such as family photographs, electronic equipment, and the medicine cabinet. Nothing was taken but the food. Investigators found a tuft of long reddish brown hair that had become caught in the corner joint of kitchen countertop. Later analysis identified the hair as *being human*. It would be interesting to know what modern-day blood typing and DNA tests might reveal from that hair sample.

In 1972 a group of loggers in the state of Washington had just returned to their logging site with a recently repaired tire weighing over 1,000 pounds. After they wrenched the tire off the delivery truck and released it from the hoist, they took a break before mounting the tire. They were surprised by a sound like laughter coming from the woods. Turning in the direction of the sound, they saw what they estimated to be an 8-foot, 800-pound Sasquatch ambling toward them. Fleeing into the woods, the loggers observed the laughing creature lift the massive tire off the ground and carry it up a nearby hill. At the top of the hill the Sasquatch set the tire on its rim and sent it rolling back toward the camp. The tire fell over and stopped within feet of where the creature had picked it up. The Sasquatch stood at the top of the hill for some time looking down at the camp, giving one of the loggers enough time to retrieve a hunting rifle from his pickup truck. As the man took a bead on the totally exposed target, he found that he could not in good conscience pull the trigger. As he lowered his rifle, the Sasquatch raised one arm and waved, then disappeared into the forest.

A young woman walking near a stream of water not far from her rural Oregon home heard sounds like low moans coming from the stream bank just ahead and to her right. Moving in the direction of the sound, she came upon a female Sasquatch in the process of childbirth. The woman watched the birth take place and had eye contact with the new mother as the latter used her tongue, stream water, and grass to clean her new arrival. The Sasquatch mother did not seem to fear the presence of the woman, and after a short period of nursing her baby she carried it across the stream, turning once to face the woman before walking into the timber.

When thinking of this type of human-Sasquatch interaction, I am reminded of a finely executed drawing (now in my slide collection) depicting a Sasquatch sitting on its haunches holding a child's small rag doll and mournfully looking at a distant log cabin as smoke rises from its chimney into a winter sky.

In about 1967 Sasquatch hunter Roger Patterson and a companion jumped from their frightened, bolting horses. Patterson grabbed an 8mm movie camera from his saddlebags and began to film before he even got his camera to eye level. After a short scene of the side of his skittish horse he focused in on a creature covered from head to toe with dark brown hair. The processed film showed a female creature (obvious by the fact it had large, swinging breasts) walking across a stream, looking back over her shoulder occasionally before disappearing.

The Patterson film has been viewed and analyzed by scientists of several appropriate disciplines. They all point to the fact that the pictures reveal the movement of specific muscles and muscle groups that would normally be used for walking by such a large anthropoid. In fact, these muscle groups are the same (on a smaller scale) as those *we* use for walking. The fact that the muscles of the creature are identical but on a larger scale supports the fact that the photographed Bigfoot was real. To build these anatomically correct features into a costume and cause them to perform in a natural manner during a prolonged period of action would admittedly overtax the abilities of Hollywood's best makeup artists.

At this point I would like to point out what I have learned from extraterrestrial contacts about the Sasquatch and their worldwide relatives.

To begin with, biomental conditions on planet Earth are not the best they could be. This is due to the fact that when the 5th planet of our solar system (called Maldek) exploded, the Earth experienced a shock wave that caused its molten core to vibrate erratically. In turn the vibrations from the core detrimentally affected the brain functions of the then-resident humans and also caused their bodies to mutate biologically. *The surviving humans were the first type of Sasquatch.* In other words, the Earth's erratic core vibrations caused human mutations, and the surviving population was reduced to hairy 4-1/2-foot creatures that used very primitive thought processes. In addition, the mutants sought shelter in trees and later in caves.

Apes and monkeys are descendants of human ancestors that were alien and not native to Earth. Because their genetics were alien, they were unsuccessful in reevolving into more human forms.

Because the vibrations from the Earth's core prevented the survivors from using higher brain-wave frequencies in their thought processes and perceptual abilities, the detrimental vibrations are called the Frequency Barrier.

Since the explosion of Maldek the Earth has been steadily healing itself by way of earthquakes, tectonic plate movements and volcanic eruptions. As the planet heals, the Frequency Barrier becomes less intense. And from the Barrier's beginning to the present, human ability to use higher mental frequencies has been increasing progressively. When the Frequency Barrier eventually disappears, humans of this planet will regain access to mental powers that we can only dream of at this time.

The extraterrestrials that operate the spacecraft we call UFOs have been monitoring earthquakes and such for thousands of years in order to determine the positive progress of the Frequency Barrier and its effects on life on Earth, particularly human life.

The visiting extraterrestrials are also human. The average height of the male is 8 feet and weighs about 750 pounds. Over the years Earthmen considered to be oddities have grown to as much as 11 feet. As the Frequency Barrier diminishes in strength we will begin to see taller individuals that will pass the height established by our present-day 7-foot basketball players.

Because the extraterrestrials were born and raised outside the effects of the Frequency Barrier, they have greater mental powers than we do.

They live in what is called an "open mental state" and we live in a "closed mental state."

The extraterrestrials must vibrate their spacecraft like a tuning fork in order to protect themselves from the detrimental effects of the Barrier. Failing to do so will result in drastic physical mutations and the loss of a great deal of their mental ability.

This brings us to the fact that there are two types of Sasquatch, the first type being those that are mutated survivors or descendants of mutated survivors of a crashed spaceship. The second type of unfortunates were deliberately marooned in the Frequency Barrier for the sake of biological experimentation.

When an extraterrestrial mutates, he or she retains its height, but will grow hair all over his/her body similar to the way our earliest ancestors did at the beginning of the Frequency Barrier. This hair growth is due to hormone imbalance. This type of imbalance is observed by the fact that a woman allergic to ether, for instance, will grow facial hair. (P.T. Barnum used ether to maintain the facial hair of his "bearded" ladies.)

The evidence points to the fact that these giant creatures reside in remote areas that are somewhat difficult to traverse and difficult to search. Some suggest that the creatures have taken to these areas to escape the encroachment of our civilization. This is somewhat true of crash survivors of earlier times, but not for the victims of experimentation. The latter are placed in these remote areas for periods of time and then picked up to study the effects of exposure to the Frequency Barrier during their stay on Earth.

1. **What do Sasquatch eat?**
2. **Are they vegetarians, carnivores, or both, as we are?**
3. **Why is the population of these creatures so low?**
4. **Do they have a high mortality rate prior to maturity?**
5. **How long do they live?**
6. **How do they cope with the seasons such as winter?**
7. **Do they hibernate?**
8. **Do they live together in families or clans, or live alone and forage as do bears, coming together only to mate?**
9. **If the Indian legends are true, why have the Sasquatch given up their tribal ways?**

The answer to questions 1 and 2: Beyond the anecdotal evidence given above, the experimental specimens are fed at different remote locations, thus keeping the hungry close to a particular area for eventual pickup. Whatever they eat, it must be of considerable daily volume to provide energy for their tremendous size.

Some of the answers to questions 3 to 9 vary as to the nature of the extraterrestrial experimenters and the type of biological experiment they were conducting.

Question 3: Females were probably artificially inseminated and then left on Earth until the gestation period was completed and birth occurred. Thus the offspring's genetics during fetal growth would be influenced by the ever-changing Frequency Barrier. The population of the Sasquatch is now limited to needs of the experimenters.

Questions 4 and 5: Extraterrestrial mutants (first generation, depending on initial age) can live up to 20 years on the Earth; second generation, possibly a few years longer. Infant mortality prevails totally from the third generation on.

Questions 6 and 7: The Sasquatch need not worry about the harshness of winter, for most likely they will be picked up for study prior to the time nature takes its toll and deprives the extraterrestrial experimenters of their biological data.

Questions 8 and 9: Most reported sightings are of individual Sasquatch. That is, rarely are two or more seen together. Older Indian legends state that the Sasquatch lived in tribes or groups just as they did. In days past, groups of crash survivors did live together until they either wasted away or were taken off the Earth by benign extraterrestrials. The Indians timidly avoided the Sasquatch that they chanced upon, fearing them to have supernatural powers.

Why would anyone want to conduct such gruesome experiments? The answer to this question is simple: One type of extraterrestrial wants to create a mutant army of surrogates (not necessarily in Sasquatch form) that can serve them in many ways from within the Frequency Barrier. They would expect these custom-made (mentally tempered and superior to us) individuals to do their bidding until the Frequency Barrier totally disappears and they themselves can come to Earth unharmed.

This type of extraterrestrial operated a genetics laboratory underground near Dulce, New Mexico, from sometime in the early 1930s to about 1948. This laboratory came into other hands thereafter, but not before a number of horrible experiments in genetic manipulation, some of which have escaped into our environment. There will be more about the Dulce base in a future article.

There is a second type of extraterrestrial that is successfully opposing this experimentation. They recommend that if you meet a Sasquatch, do not harm him/her; after loudly speaking the words, "Have doe me kale done soc" (I witness your presence; I am a friend), turn and slowly leave the area.

People's World Report, April 15, 1991, tells of a capture of a 560-pound, 7-foot-tall Bigfoot that was brought down with a tranquilizer dart near Helena, Montana. The report relates that after regaining consciousness, the creature has thus far been uncommunicative. We have yet to hear the end of this astonishing occurrence. Hopefully the full story will be forthcoming and reveal the fact that Bigfoot is real and is truly part of our ancient ancestry—and part of the formulation of our unknown future.

2.

The Finding of Flight 19

June 1991

The loss of Flight 19 on December 5, 1945, is a classic disappearance that took place in the Bermuda Triangle. It began with a routine training flight participated in by five Grumman Avenger torpedo bombers, also known as TBMs. The planes on the mission were designated Flight 19. Their radio identification code was the letters F-T.

It is reported that 4 of the TBMs carried crews of 3 men and one carried a crew of 2. Thus the flight consisted of 14 men.

While returning to their base at Fort Lauderdale Naval Air Station, the flight leader Lt. Charles C. Taylor radioed back to the base that the flight was in some kind of trouble. Apparently they were lost, and the confusion continued for about an hour, after which the radio signals grew weaker and weaker until they disappeared. The 5 planes and 14 men aboard them were then reported missing.

During the hour of confusion it is reported that the following radio conversation took place between Lt. Taylor and the Fort Lauderdale tower:

Taylor: "Calling control tower...emergency. We seem to have gone off course... we can't see the ground any more. I repeat: we can't see the ground."

Another reporting source states that this transmission included the statement: "We can't see the ground or the sun."

Tower: "What is your position?"

Taylor: "We are not certain of our position. We don't know exactly where we are; we seem to be lost."

Tower: "In that case, you must fly west."

Taylor: "We can't tell which is west. Nothing is working properly. It's nuts... we can't be sure of any direction. Even the sea looks funny...."

It then became more difficult to pick up messages from Flight 19. The aircraft progressively lost contact with the tower, but every now and then snatches of conversation between the pilots were heard. They were discussing the possibility of running out of fuel, of 75-knot winds, of malfunctioning magnetic and gyro compasses.

According to some reports, the last words heard from Flight 19 were: "We are entering white water. We are completely lost."

Reporter Art Ford stated that another radio conversation took place between flight leader Taylor and a fellow Navy pilot Lt. F. Cox, who was in the air but not part of Flight 19. The conversation went as follows:

Cox: "What is your altitude? I will fly south to meet you."

Taylor: "Don't come after me. They look like they're from outer space. Don't come after me!"

The text of these and all other radio transmissions from Flight 19 are on public record in the National Archives in Washington D.C.

One report states that Taylor was overheard to either turn over the command of the flight to another pilot in the formation, or turn over the flying duties of his plane. This is not clear.

It is also reported that one of the Avenger pilots broke formation and took off on his own to find safer and more familiar skies.

The fact that the compasses and radios of all five planes malfunctioned at the same time and that Lt. Taylor did not comply with the constant request that he switch his radio to the emergency frequency adds to the mystery.

Fort Lauderdale sent a Martin Mariner (a large amphibious craft) to try to rescue the five Avengers. There were 13 men aboard the Mariner.

One hour after take-off the Martin Mariner disappeared, too. The control tower tried in vain to contact its pilot. What happened to the Martin Mariner?

A little after 7 p.m., the Naval Air Station at Opalocka picked up an almost inaudible radio signal that continually repeated "FT...FT," which was the call sign of Flight 19. Could this have been a communication from the Avengers?

Nothing was found of the 5 TBMs or the Mariner, in spite of the intensive search by 240 land-based aircraft, 70 aircraft from the aircraft carrier Solomons, 4 destroyers, 18 Coast Guard patrol boats, hundreds of private aircraft and yachts and boats of all sorts. Nothing was found: no inflatable rafts, not the least trace of oil, not a sign of wreckage. Avenger-type aircraft are known to float from minutes to hours. Why were no bodies, oil slicks or wreckage of any type found? Why didn't any of the men use their parachutes and life rafts?

During the search of December 6, 1945, a Navy Privateer, which was a 1-tail version of the Army Air Corps 2-tail B-24, also disappeared without a trace.

A report published by the Navy after several months of inquiry offered no explanation for the disappearances.

During the evening of August 16, 1985, I was engaged in assembling and combining videotape segments that contained accounts and pictures pertaining to the subject of UFOs. I combined three videotape segments, which were:

1. A series of computer enhancements of a Swiss Air Force jet that had been photographed along with a UFO.

2. The account of the missing five TBM (Grumman Avenger torpedo bombers) and a Martin Mariner (seaplane) in the Bermuda Triangle.

3. UFO photographs and motion picture footage that was taken by American astronauts as they conducted missions in space.

The videotape from which I was dubbing segment 3 was several years old and had not been played recently. On several occasions during the dubbing process, the player deck misidentified the original recording speed of the tape. This caused the tape to slow down, distorting parts of the dub. To accomplish my work, I had to run the tape over and over again until the problem cleared up.

During these numerous reruns my attention was drawn to a picture of an odd-shaped UFO that was photographed by the crew of Apollo 11 on July 16, 1969, while they were en route to the first moon landing.

Even though the shape of this UFO was irregular, it looked familiar to me. I knew I had seen that shape before. I soon realized that I had in fact seen something similar to that shape only several minutes before when I was dubbing the segment that contained the computer-analysis pictures of the UFO and Swiss Air Force jet.

Apollo 11 UFO (Official NASA photo)

I then ran off a black-and-white photo of the Apollo 11 UFO on my video printer. After rotating the video-print from the vertical to the horizontal, I concluded that the UFO had the shape of an ***airplane that was either encased in ice or some other material.***

Following the contour of the UFO from nose to tail, I noted the familiar blunt nose and long canopy that covered the two-seat cockpit, the bubble of the rear gun turret, and the high tail of the Grumman TBM Avenger torpedo bomber.

Apollo 11 UFO (Enlarged and rotated)

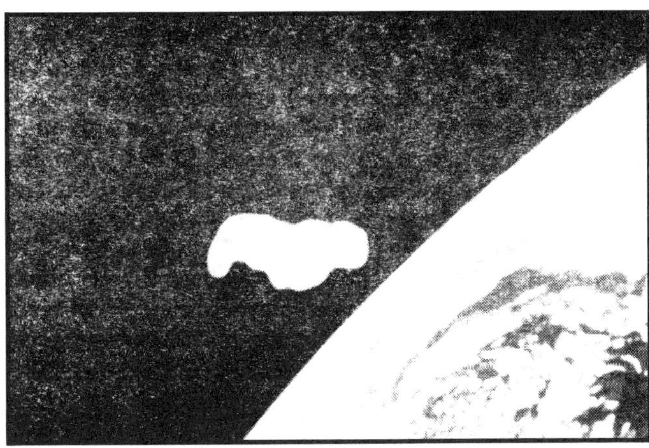

Returning to the segment that pertained to the missing planes (Flight 19) I made a video photo of an Avenger for comparison with the Apollo UFO. This comparison left me in little doubt that the Apollo 11 UFO was the remains of a Grumman Avenger and most likely one of the five that once composed Flight 19.

In studying the Apollo UFO, two things about the shape of the object bothered me. (1) The tail looked a little too close to the rear gun turret. (2) There are two small arclike indentations in the bottom of the object just below the position of the cockpit.

Both of these questions were answered by a friend who at one time flew this type of plane when dropping borate on forest fires.

There are two possible answers for the tail appearing to be too close to the rear turret. (1) The angle from which the astronauts took the

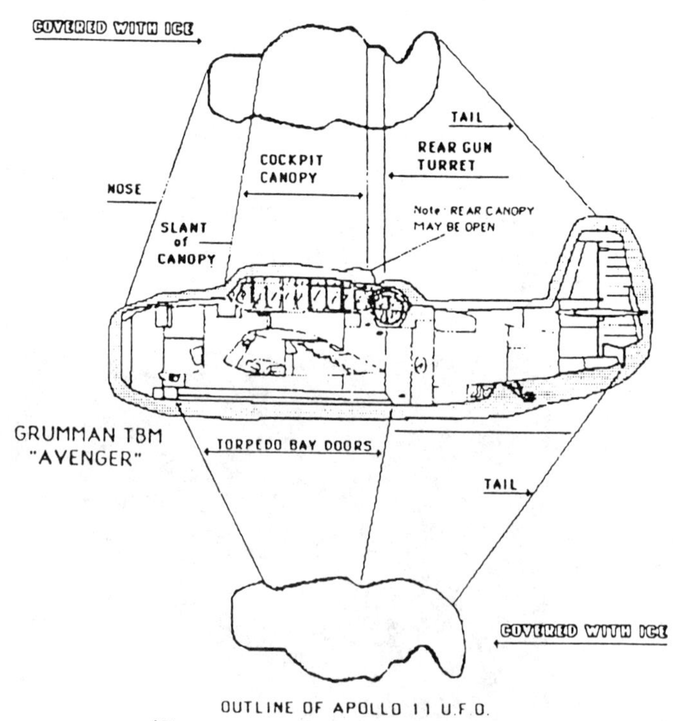

Computer print by Wes Bateman

fuselage is bent at an angle due to the tail section hitting the waters of the Atlantic in what my friend called a "boomerang crash." From personal knowledge he said that it was common for an Avenger that crashes into the sea to end up with a bent rear fuselage.

My friend then answered the question of the existing arclike indentations in the belly of the plane/UFO. His answer was simple: The indentations represent either the collapsed torpedo bombing doors or their absence.

The silhouette (shadow) of a scale-model TBM was superimposed over a slide projection of the Apollo UFO, ***finding that all features fit exactly.***

The Apollo 11 UFO photo was taken when the spacecraft was one day out en route to the moon. I have not ascertained what distance Apollo 11 was from the earth when the photo was taken.

One thing is quite certain; the Avenger in the astronaut's photo did not and could not attain orbital velocity and insert itself into any orbit, let alone an orbit that ranged far out into space. This, of course, means that something natural, supernatural, or man-made that had these physical abilities in 1945 placed at least one of the missing five planes into earth orbit.

One explanation is that some freak natural force such as a giant tornado-like vortex sucked up the Avengers and accelerated them to a speed in excess of 18,000 miles an hour (gravitational escape velocity). Another explanation is that some power source planted by some sort of intelligence went into action either by plan or chance. Both are somewhat discredited by the communication Lt. Taylor had with Lt. Cox: "Don't come after me. They look like they're from outer space. Don't come after me!" From Lt. Taylor's words we can conclude that he might have been encountering at the time more than one something (thus the plural terms "they" and "they're" in his communication). Then again he may have had sight of one thing that he thought contained a number of occupants who in his opinion were demonstrating something he was sure was not of this world.

It is reported that the planes were armed and their mission actually entailed dropping explosives into the sea. If this is true, this activity might have triggered the fate of the airmen involved.

Perhaps in the course of their bombing they accidently hit and damaged a submerged alien spacecraft – or maybe they had actually been sent on a mission to target the spacecraft. If the latter is true, you can bet the Navy will never admit it.

Let's for the moment imagine that the Avengers were either deliberately or accidently drawn into a force field that relates to a field-drive propulsion system of the damaged extraterrestrial spacecraft. Such a field-drive system might have some active electromagnetic components and gravitational effects, which in turn would account for the malfunctioning of the magnetic and gyro compasses of the Avengers, causing Lt. Taylor to say: "We can't tell which is west. Nothing is working properly. It's nuts.. .we can't be sure of any direction. Even the sea looks funny...."

It is safe to speculate that at least 1 of the 4 Avengers (or 5, counting the one that reportedly left the flight formation) were drawn into the vortex of a spacecraft's propulsion system (as birds are sometimes drawn into jet engines). After that maybe other things – such as large volumes of foaming seawater –were also drawn into the spacecraft's field drive, causing Lt. Taylor to transmit the statement: *"We are entering white water. We are completely lost!"*

It is possible that Lt. Taylor did comply with the request to switch his radio to the emergency frequency, but perhaps radio waves of that frequency could not escape the confines of the spacecraft's field drive.

At this point we can imagine the extraterrestrial spacecraft accelerating into space, either in ignorance of or with full knowledge that they were dragging with them 1 or more of the 5 Avengers plus large amounts of seawater.

Such an ascent must have been quite rapid, and by the time the spacecraft reached outer space the Avenger pilots would be dead, entombed in their planes now sheathed in frozen seawater.

Upon reaching outer space, the Avengers, now having acquired a velocity that would permit them to orbit the earth (for at least 24 years) were either jettisoned by the spacecraft or released automatically when the spacecraft changed its propulsion field for the purpose of space travel. In either case the Avengers could have been dropped off at intervals that might now separate them in the same orbit or in successively higher orbits by thousands of miles.

When the question of why the extraterrestrials would do such a thing is considered, many thoughts come to mind:

(1) Their actions might represent a disregard for the lives of what they might consider to be a lower life form. (2) Their encounter and involvement with Flight 19 might have been an accident caused by a malfunction of their propulsion system or by damage to the system sustained from bombs dropped unknowingly or deliberately by the Avengers on the spaceship(s) lying submerged in the sea. If the Avengers did not practice live bombing runs that day, perhaps their practice attack dives could have been interpreted by the extraterrestrials as a real threat.

I prefer to think that the Martin Mariner and the Privateer became lost for different, unrelated reasons, because the alternative implies that they were deliberately destroyed or captured by the extraterrestrials out of revenge.

Returning to the subject of the Apollo 11 UFO, the photograph indicates that the plane might have "boomerang crashed" into the sea, thus bending its fuselage at an angle. This could be the only plane of Flight 19 that is in orbit. It could very well be the plane that left the formation.

In this possible scenario, four of the Avengers and their crews are taken aboard the extraterrestrial spacecraft intact, and the fifth plane and its crew are fished from the sea. Later the plane and maybe its crew are abandoned in orbit.

In the spring of 1990, a supermarket tabloid headlined: "World War Two Bomber Found on the Moon." An accompanying picture provided by a Soviet space probe showed a U.S. Navy Privateer resting in a lunar crater. Is this the Privateer that disappeared while looking for the 5 TBMs and the Mariner?

It is hopeful to think that all the men of Flight 19 are now alive and well on some distant world, learning all they can about the culture and technology of their extraterrestrial hosts. Some day they might return in the manner depicted in the motion picture *Close Encounters of the Third Kind* and tell us what really happened on that day some 40 years ago.

Nolan Luftus of Salt Lake City, Utah, was an employee of McDonnell-Douglas and was present at Mission Control during the Apollo 11 mission. His first-hand account of the Apollo UFO sighting and photography by the spacecraft's crew is as follows:

"The UFO was in orbit at about a 6000- mile altitude. At first the

Apollo crew thought that it was their discarded booster rocket, but it was later proven that this rocket stage was some 6000 miles away at the time. The booster rocket was about forty feet long [which is the same length as a TBM]."

The Apollo crew used several rolls of film to photograph the UFO. Because of the importance of the Apollo 11 mission, little was said or done about the UFO until the crew and photographs were returned to earth.

Even though a number of photographs of the UFO were taken, it appears that only one of the exposures has been widely circulated.

NASA's photoanalysis of the UFO initially declared the UFO to be a "formation of ice" and later stated it was a piece of debris only 10 inches long and from the Apollo spacecraft itself. NASA would have us believe that the *highly trained* Apollo astronauts' estimated 40-foot length of the object was wrong. What do *you* think?

FLIGHT 19: THE BALLAD OF CHARLIE TAYLOR

December the sixth, nineteen forty-five.
There were 14 men who were young and alive.
They flew away each and every one,
Off to the east in the Florida sun.

Lieutenant Charles Taylor led the pack
As they dove toward the ocean in a mock attack.
The 5 TBM Avengers resumed again their flight
And headed home to base before the coming night.

Charlie Taylor, Charlie Taylor, what was your fate?
Did you and your comrades have a destiny date?
Do you circle the earth again and again
Among the stars with your brave men?

Fort Lauderdale tower, we appear to be lost.
We must make it home whatever the cost.
These were Charlie's words, strange as they seem.
They add to the mystery of Flight 19.

Don't come after us, don't come to this place.
They look as if they're from outer space.
Our compasses do not work, they're out of order.
We're lost, we're lost, we're entering white water.

Charlie Taylor, Charlie Taylor, what was your fate?
Did you and your comrades have a destiny date?
Do you circle the earth again and again
Among the stars with your brave men?

Control, this is Apollo 11, we wish you to know:
Beneath us at four o'clock we see a UFO.
Cameras clicked away at the object in sight.
Then Apollo returned to its lunar flight.

Photographs taken were clear and precise,
But NASA chose to call the image orbiting ice.
At a closer look it's plain to see it's really a TBM
As flown that day by Charlie Taylor and his men.

Charlie Taylor, Charlie Taylor, what was your fate?
Did you and your comrades have a destiny date?
Do you circle the earth again and again
Among the stars with your brave men?

3
Flight 19 Update

July 1991

The June 1991 issue of the *Sedona Calendar of Creative Happenings* published both my account and NASA pictures (taken by the astronauts of Apollo 11) of what appears to be a Grumman TBM Avenger in earth orbit. As fate would have it, just prior to the publication of my article, the news media released the story of the discovery of five TBMs on the bottom of the Atlantic Ocean about 10 miles off the east coast of Florida. This discovery of five planes was prematurely taken to be the remains of Flight 19.

Because the wreckage was thought to be from the lost flight, my article about the orbiting TBM appeared to some readers as having no merit. Other readers suggested that if the orbiting object were an airplane, it might not necessarily be one of those from Flight 19.

On June 4, 1991, both Channel 10 (KTSP) in Phoenix, Arizona, and the Cable News Network (CNN) both reported that the recently discovered planes were "**definitely not part of Flight 19**."

This returns us to the strong possibility that the UFO picture(s) taken by the Apollo 11 astronauts on their way to the first moon landing was one of the TBMs from Flight 19. I closed my June article on the orbiting TBM with the question: "What do you think?" I'll leave you now with the same question.

4

The Secret Of The Flying Saucers

July 1991

Flying Saucers have been visiting us for thousands of years. During the reign of the Pharaoh Thutmoses III (ruler of Egypt about 1500 B.C.), his scribes wrote: "In the year 22 and the third month of winter a circle of fire came out of the sky. Later it was joined by other circles of fire. When the pharaoh ordered his army to assemble around him, the circles flew skyward and disappeared." This account is found in what is called the Tulli Papyrus, which is reproduced below.

From the Tulli Papyrus

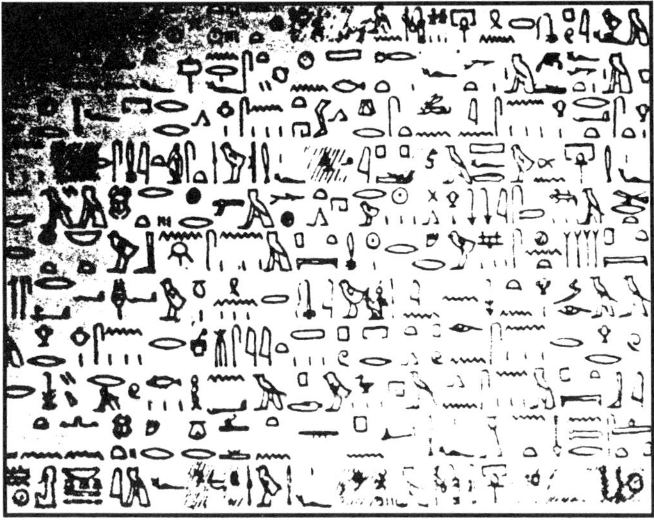

During the time of the Roman Empire and later during the Middle Ages a great number of UFO sightings were documented.

In today's technology we have devices that could be used to map and totally analyze a distant planet in one 5-day mission — that is, if we had a spacecraft that could carry all the required instruments to that planet. But we don't.

The question is: If these strange objects are in reality extraterrestrial spacecraft, why have their operators been coming to Earth again and again for centuries? They are certainly long finished with mapping and analyzing this planet. The answer to this question is obvious: They are observing something that is constantly changing, something we on Earth are totally unaware of.

Interest in Nuclear Facilities

In the mid-1940s UFOs were often spotted at locations where we were testing our nuclear bombs and guided missiles. Theories arose suggesting that the extraterrestrials were concerned about our nuclear testing and/or our development of nuclear weapons.

Extraterrestrials are interested in nuclear bomb tests only because those detonations produce effects similar to those produced by a natural phenomenon they have been observing long before nuclear bombs ever existed. This natural phenomenon is, of course, *earthquakes.*

Earthquakes and UFOs

In the year 224 B.C. the Roman historian Pliny wrote that there were fiery chariots and shining shields that were seen in the sky during the destruction of the Colossus of Rhodes by a great earthquake. The Colossus, which is listed as one of the Seven Wonders of the Ancient

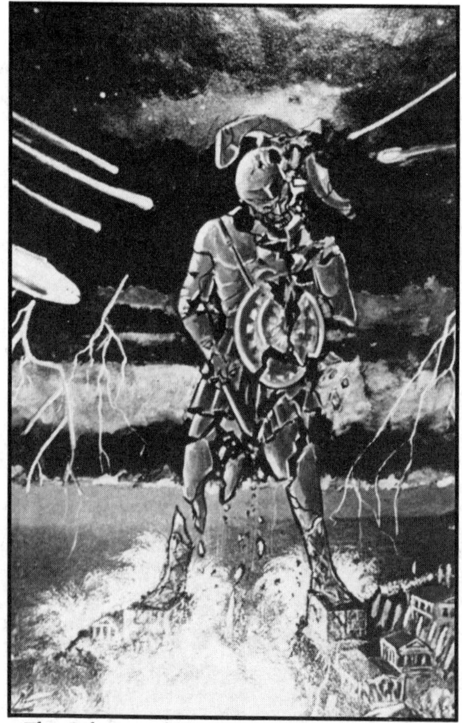

The Colossus of Rhodes and Saucers

World, was a large statue of the Greek sun god Helios. The statue, which took the Greeks 12 years to build, is said to have stood in the harbor of the island of Rhodes in such a way that ships of the time sailed between its legs.

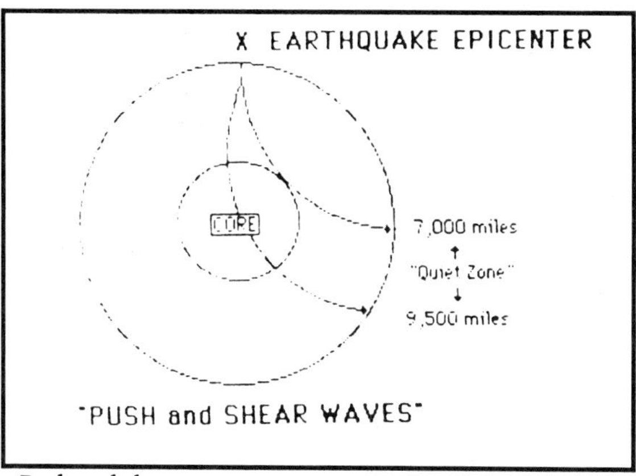

Push and shear waves

Earthquakes occur when energy builds up in rock layers that compose an earthquake fault. Eventually the energy causes heavy stress in the rock layers and causes them to move (slip) or break, and therefore generate waves of energy that radiate out in every direction from the epicenter. Some of these waves move straight out from the earthquake's epicenter. Others move in the same direction but also side to side like a crawling serpent. These waves are called, respectively, push and shear waves (sometimes primary and secondary waves, or simply P and S waves).

Most push and shear waves penetrate the Earth. Some bounce (deflect) off the planet's molten core. Others pass through the core, as depicted below.

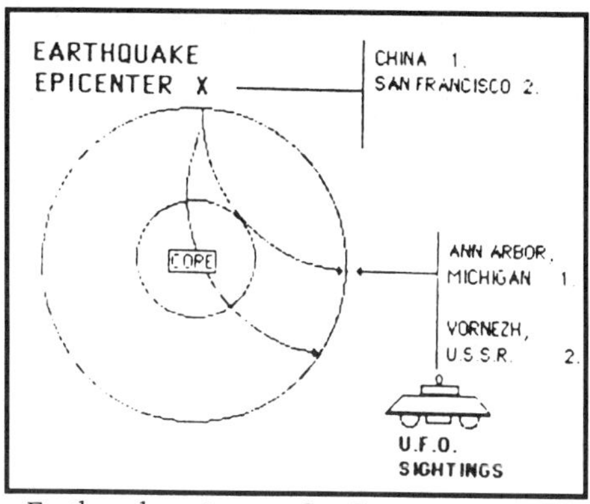

Earthquake epicenter, San Francisco

The strongest push and shear waves reflect off the Earth's core and emerge (resurface) at points 7,000 miles surface distance from the earthquake's epicenter. Push and shear waves that pass through the core are weakened in the process. These waves resurface about 9,500 miles surface distance from the earthquake's epicenter.

On March 20, 21 and 22, 1966, the *Los Angeles Herald Examiner* carried double headlines proclaiming the occurrence of massive earthquakes in China and UFO sightings that took place at Ann Arbor and Hillsdale, Michigan.

In October 1989 a devastating earthquake occurred in San Francisco, California. Several days prior to this quake, newspapers and television reported a UFO landing at Voronezh, a city about 300 miles south of Moscow.

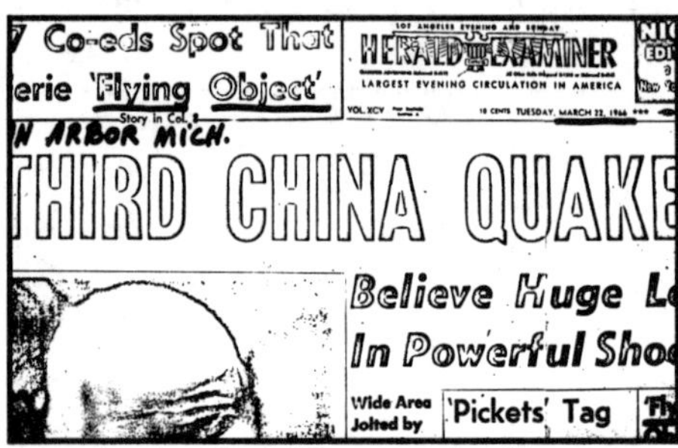
Co-eds Spot That
erie 'Flying Object'
Story in Col.
N ARBOR MICH.
HERALD EXAMINER
LARGEST EVENING CIRCULATION IN AMERICA
THIRD CHINA QUAK
Believe Huge L
In Powerful Sho
Wide Area Jolted by
'Pickets' Tag

Los Angeles Herald Examiner headlines

The illustration on the previous page reveals that the UFO sightings correspond to points on the globe at which the strongest push and shear waves resurface and can be analyzed by the extraterrestrials.

In the fall of 1968 a Fort Lauderdale, Florida newspaper carried articles side by side on the same page titled "Fiery Objects seen in New York Skies" and "Philadelphia Shaken by Quake."

On October 5, 1973, the *Orange County* (California) *Register* carried the headline "Huge Dixie UFO: Law Officers Describe Sighting." Then on October 6, 1973, the Long Beach, California, *Independent* carried the headline "Huge Chile Quake."

The Register
MID-DAY EDITION
METROPOLITAN ORANGE COUNTY'S NEWSPAPER
HUGE DIXIE UFO
Law Officers Decribe Sighting
NEWS
LATE SPORTS
INDEPENDENT 10¢
FINA

Register and Independent headlines

Over a period of several days prior to the Chilean quake of October 6, 1973, the southeastern part of the United States was blanketed with UFO activity.

During this UFO activity, then-Governor of the state of Georgia, Jimmy Carter, and ten others reported seeing a UFO in the skies over Leary, Georgia.

Most of the UFO sightings of October 1973 took place in the vicinity of the New Madrid fault line. A moderate earthquake did occur as the saucers winged about. This quake took place on a part of the fault that seismologists previously thought was inactive. This, of course, means

UFO over southern States

that the extraterrestrials can predict when and where an earthquake is going to take place. This is confirmed by the following account as well.

A series of phenomenal UFO pictures were taken by Agusto Arranda at Yungay, Peru, in the late 1960s. Within a year of this UFO activity at Yungay, the town was wiped off the face of the map by a tremendous earthquake and mudslide. The Yungay disaster is considered the greatest natural catastrophe ever to occur in the Western Hemisphere and is in the top 10 of all the disasters that ever occurred in the world.

The picture below is of the

The El Tannin

United States Science Foundation research ship, the *El Tannin*. The vessel was specially designed and built for the foundation's Antarctic research program. While conducting underwater photography 1,000 miles west of Cape Horn along the major fault line that circles the Earth, a picture was taken of a strange device resting next to the fault at a depth of 13,000 feet. The device had an antenna with crossbars similar to a telemetry antenna. The scientists aboard the *El Tannin* were puzzled as to what function the device had and who on earth produced the technology to build such a device that could withstand the crushing pressures that exist at those depths. It apparently never occurred to the El Tannin scientists that they had accidently taken a picture of an extraterrestrial seismographic device.

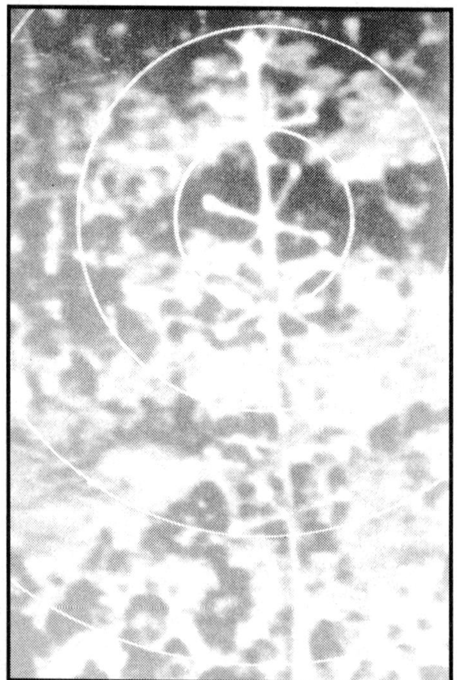

The device photographed by the El Tannin on the ocean floor. Taken from the cover of "Harmonic 33" by Bruce Cathie.

The extraterrestrials had to take nuclear bomb detonations into account since the mid-1940s if they were to continue with their ages-old studies of push and shear waves as they pass through our planet.

From Jackass Flats to Tashkent

In the 1960s the United States conducted high-yield underground nuclear bomb detonations at Jackass Flats, Nevada. These tests produced push and shear waves that resurfaced in the vicinity of Tashkent, a city in the Uzbek region of the Soviet Union. These waves contributed energy to a fault line in the area that eventually gave way to a series of massive earthquakes.

Soviet underground tests conducted in Siberia contribute energy to fault lines in Turkey, Armenia and Afghanistan. The faults in these areas need very little unnatural encouragement, as they frequently give way during natural quakes.

From New Mexico to India

In 1968 a nuclear device was set off at Farmington, New Mexico. The project was called Gas Buggy and was intended to exploit a natural gas pocket in the area. Within two minutes of the detonation at Farmington, push and shear waves from the blast triggered an earthquake in India that killed about 200 people. Such a quake would have eventually happened naturally, but the waves from the nuclear detonation hastened it along.

It has long been evident that underground nuclear tests are really tests (or were tests) of a weapon system that employed push and shear waves as a means of destruction. If properly aimed, a high-yield underground nuclear detonation could lift a city 7,000 miles away a foot into the air, only to have it resettle in ruins. This type of system would not need costly intercontinental missiles to deliver destruction. The devastated country of the enemy could be immediately occupied, as there would be no hazardous radioactivity present at the target sites.

The extraterrestrials are also interested in volcanic eruptions, as they too generate push and shear waves. On different days just prior to the most recent eruption of Mount St. Helens, triangular-shaped UFOs were spotted and reported only a few miles west of the mountain.

Why have the extraterrestrials been interested in the push-and-shear waves produced by earthquakes, nuclear bomb detonations and volcanic eruptions? What is so fascinating about this phenomenon? Why have they put thousands of years of time and effort into studying it? This question will be answered in next month's issue of *Sedona Creative Happenings*. Don't miss it.

5
The Frequency Barrier

August 1991

ET Interest in Seismic Activity

It is obvious that the extraterrestrials have an interest in seismic waves that are generated by earthquakes, volcanic eruptions and nuclear bomb detonations. It is also obvious that they have been studying these waves for thousands of years. The question is, why?

The answer to this question was acquired by way of telepathic communication between the visiting extraterrestrials and certain individuals that are *physically but not psychically* native to this planet.

Solar System Teemed with Life Long Ago

The extraterrestrials state that in the very distant past many of the planets of this solar system or at least one or more of a particular planet's moons were *teeming with life, including human life.* This may be somewhat hard to accept, given the nonlife conditions of the planets that have been reported by our space probes. Among the nonlife data there is a glimmer of evidence that suggests that intelligent human life existed on the planet Mars some 500,000 years ago. This evidence is in the form of photographs taken of that planet by an orbiting Viking space vehicle. The pictures show a number of pyramids and what appear to be other types of structures. The most impressive of the artifacts that are located at a place called Cydonia is a large human face that is more than a mile long and about 1500 feet high.

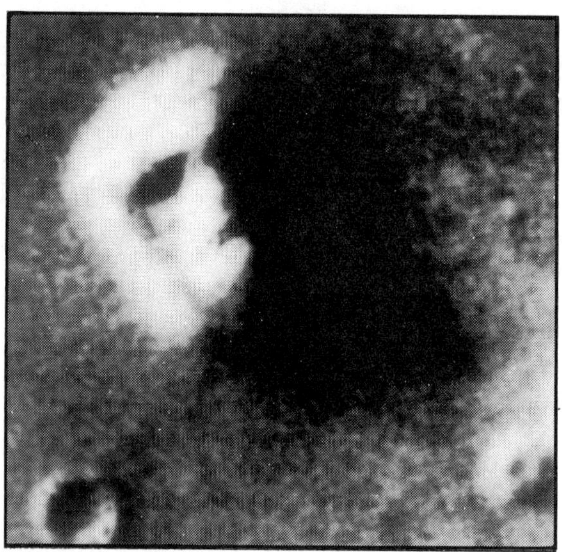
Face on Mars

At one time the Earth had only one continent that was surrounded by a shallow ocean (compared to present ocean depths). The waters of the Earth were atomically pure (not containing the hydrogen isotope deuterium). The native population (Elder Race) of the Earth was never greater than 40 million people.

If a man of the Elder Race were compared to a man of today, there would be several remarkable differences. A man of the Elder Race was about 8 feet tall and had mental abilities that today we could only refer to as extrasensory. Some evidence of this ancient civilization has survived in the form of a gigantic human shin bone that was found in lava strata estimated to be 6 million years old and a machine screw found in an anthracite coal deposit also estimated to be millions of years old. In addition, a tile floor was found in ancient strata in the state of Montana. A machined metal object was unearthed in a deep mine in Hungary. And a geode found in Death Valley, California, when cut in two revealed a machined object resembling a modern spark plug. From time to time finds of petrified giant human remains are reported, with little or nothing said about them at any later time.

In those earliest of days, space travelers from the nearby planets and from other solar systems visited the Earth, and people of this planet (by means of the technology of others) also made excursions into the universe.

Maldek, the 5th Planet, and the Maldekian Incursion

Over a period of time the people of the Elder Race came to admire the people of the fifth planet of this system. This planet was called Maldek. The Maldekians were fair-skinned blondes that had a "fast lane" attitude about life and deliberately inspired primal psychic excitement in those they came in contact with. Eventually, the Maldekians began to govern the populations of the Earth whom they later subjected and enslaved.

The Traveling Pyramid Builders

During the time of the Maldekian rule of the Earth, a group of people originating outside this solar system first suggested and then contracted the construction of pyramids on the order of the "sacred geometry" that is used by nature. This group then provided both the expertise and the labor to build these structures on Mars and elsewhere in the solar system. The Maldekians saw that such buildings could be used to perform certain physical functions that in turn would permit them to expand their power and influence throughout the stars, so they invited the pyramid builders to come to Earth.

Egypt Had the Strongest Vortex

Planet Earth, as any other planet, has spots on its surface at which a certain type of energy will concentrate. These spots are known as a vortex and to the American Indians as a Medicine Wheel. The type of energy that concentrates at a vortex is called *vril* energy, which is the energy of creation. It is from a matrix of vril energy concentrated at a vortex spot that every living thing was first manifested into third-dimensional reality, thereafter to multiply by procreation. The center of the biggest and strongest vortex on the Earth during the Maldekian rule was located at what is now called the Giza plateau in Egypt.

Commissioning the Great Pyramid

The Maldekians commissioned the construction of the Great Pyramid of Giza, a monument whose construction was later wrongfully credited to King Khufu of the fourth dynasty of ancient Egypt. The Maldekians had three purposes for building the Great Pyramid and placing it in the center of the Earth's largest and strongest vortex. (1) The first was to use the pyramid to concentrate the vril energy of the vortex (in which the pyramid stood) to a greater degree than its natural degree of concentration and strength. (2) They wanted to use this concentrated energy to biologically alter human genes and splice them to those of different animals. This was a deliberate attempt to violate the Master Plan of the Universe. A successful physical violation of the Master Plan would elevate the violators to an equality with God the Creator. (At least that's what they thought at the time and what other extraterrestrials of this day still believe). (3) The third purpose the Maldekians had for the Great Pyramid was to use it as a transmitter of the Earth's vril energy. They wanted to steal this energy from the Earth and transmit it to their home planet. If such a scheme had worked, no planet's energy would have been safe from them.

The labor force that built the Great Pyramid also built several other pyramids in Egypt and elsewhere. The builders based themselves in a city of their own design now identified as the pre-Columbian city of Teotihuacan, Mexico. This city was excavated and occupied thousands of years later by Indian civilizations that saw no reason for the impressive pyramids and living quarters to go to waste. The surviving ancient pyramids and buildings of Egypt were also utilized and even poorly copied.

Maldekians' Biological Experiment

Upon completion of the Great Pyramid, the Maldekians began their biological experiments symbolized by the form of the Sphinx that stands close to the pyramid and is sculpted to resemble the head of a man with the body of a lion. The Maldekians on one fateful day also began to transmit the Earth's creative energy (vril energy) to their own planet.

Maldek's Destruction

The planet Maldek at first was very receptive to this energy; then it began to "shudder." Buildings began to topple. Suddenly, the planet exploded into pieces. What happened is similar to a singer sounding a musical note and breaking a glass goblet. The shattered remains of Maldek then took up solar orbits between the planets Mars and Jupiter. The chunks of debris are now called the asteroid belt.

Every planet in the solar system suffered in one way or another from the destruction of Maldek. Planets such as Mars became uninhabitable. On Mars, geological conditions that scientists here estimate should take millions of years to develop in fact took only hundreds of thousands of years. An artificial moon called Phoebus had to be placed in orbit around Mars to stabilize its orbit and keep it from spiraling into the Sun.

Aftereffects on Earth

The Earth, on the other hand, suffered a much different fate. The vril energy transmitted by the Great Pyramid fed back to the Earth like microphone feedback into a speaker. This feedback caused the Earth's molten core to begin to vibrate erratically. Within four years after

Maldek's destruction, the Earth's core was vibrating at a tremendous rate. The single continent of the planet and certain key strata that made up the continent's base cracked and began to separate. This was accompanied by violent electrical storms, earthquakes and volcanic eruptions.

Compared to the many buildings that cover the Earth today (to serve the present-day population of billions), the relatively small population of ancient Earth had very few metropolitan areas of any notable size. What they did have was destroyed by the catastrophic events following the explosion of Maldek. Surprisingly, only a few of those structures built using sacred geometry have survived to date.

Earth's Absorption of Deuterium

Earth at one point in time passed in its orbit through a large hydrogen cloud that formed due to the explosion of Maldek. This cloud interacted with the Earth's rich oxygen atmosphere and electrical storm activity, and formed enough water to fill our oceans to their present depths. The difference in the then newly created water was that it contained the isotope of hydrogen called deuterium. The extraterrestrials say that it is the deuterium in our water that causes us to age.

Results of Earth's Core Vibration

Any native humans or extraterrestrial visitors on the planet that lived through the upheaval of the Earth then mutated. Their immediate descendants began to get smaller in size and became covered with hair. The once supermental abilities (extrasensory) of the Elder Race were lost, and survivors and their descendants were reduced to using only basic reasoning and animal-like instincts. This mental depletion was due to the erratic vibrations emitted from the planet's core. Because these vibrations restricted those of the Earth (in those early times) from using higher mental frequencies, the restricting core vibrations are collectively called "the frequency barrier."

Over time, extraterrestrials have related the story of the frequency barrier to persons of later cultures. One such story comes to us from the Aztec Indians of Mexico: "In earlier days the Great God Humac Ku became angry with the men of earth who were giants in stature. The God subjected the earth to fires, floods and earthquakes. Thereafter, men were shrunk in size and turned into monkeys."

Healing the Frequency Barrier

Since the beginning of the frequency barrier, earthquakes, volcanic eruptions and tectonic plate movements have been playing a part in the healing process of the Earth. Because of these phenomena the once greatly fractured key strata within the Earth are moving back together. As these key strata are progressively moved back toward their original natural positions, the frequency barrier progressively becomes less intense (less detrimental).

Since the healing process began, mankind has been reevolving back to the form and supermental abilities of our ancestors (Elder Race) and that of the extraterrestrials that are visiting our planet at the present time. There are many physical features expressed by humans that do not fit the evolutionary theory, but these physical features are easily explained by our reevolution.

We are the "missing link." Apes, chimpanzees and monkeys are really the descendants of humans of an extraterrestrial origin that could not biologically negotiate the reevolutionary conditions imposed by the frequency barrier.

Effect of Fault Lines

Over the ages humans instinctively found it comfortable to settle in the vicinity of fault lines on the Earth. As long as the fault lines were seismically active, they offered some small relief from the frequency barrier. When the faults became inactive, the civilizations near them stagnated and from that point failed to progress. This type of human effect from fault lines is seen in the present-day population concentrations along California's active San Andreas fault.

Animals are quite sensitive to impending earthquakes (changes in the frequency barrier). Some types of wild animals will leave an area days before the occurrence of an earthquake. Days before the Alaskan earthquake of 1964, bears left their hibernation dens weeks before they would have done so normally. During this same earthquake, zoos throughout the world reported that their animals became unnaturally excited. Prior to an earthquake shrimp pick up their eggs and move to dry land. Ants also attempt to move their eggs. Snakes will leave their places of winter hibernation, only to freeze to death on the winter ice.

Effect of the Full Moon

During full moon phases the moon apparently affects the frequency barrier. Many psychiatrists report that even in a darkened room mentally ill patients will react differently during different phases of the moon.

Game wardens in Africa report that during periods of high sun-spot activity (about every 11 years) elephants will start to migrate. Sun-spot activity apparently affects the frequency barrier to some degree.

Effect on Our Mental Ability

We of this day and age use only about 20% of our full mental abilities, whereas the extraterrestrials use 100%. The extraterrestrials call the mental condition in which we function the "closed mental state" and their mental environment the "open mental state." Eventually, the frequency barrier will be gone and we of the Earth will live as the extraterrestrials do in the open, unrestricted mental state.

The extraterrestrials cannot tolerate the frequency barrier if they come into it without taking certain precautions. If unprotected, they will physically mutate, become mentally defective and grow hair all over their bodies (as did our most distant ancestors). This will happen to an unprotected extraterrestrial because although we are biologically tempered for this condition, they are not. Concerning extraterrestrial frequency barrier mutations, see the article entitled "Sasquatch" in the May 1991 issue of *Sedona Creative Happenings.*

Earthquakes Affect Core's Vibration

A recent study by the Massachusetts Institute of Technology stated that one earthquake of considerable size could cause the Earth's molten core to vibrate for as long as 10,000 years. The study added that earthquakes occurring thereafter will dampen (slow down) the vibrations in the core produced by the original quake. This type of seismic activity sometimes moves the frequency barrier 3 degrees forward and 2 degrees backward.

The extraterrestrials state that since the beginning of the frequency barrier there have been a number of short-lived "golden ages" during which the frequency barrier was less intense than it is even today. During these golden ages the extraterrestrials attempted to interact and to inform certain persons about the frequency barrier. Earthquakes of considerable size occurring during these ages wiped out the physical gains and mental benefits. The Earth and its human residents were once more plunged into mental chaos.

ETs Monitoring Seismic Activity

The extraterrestrials do not expect the Earth to experience any more golden ages before the end of the frequency barrier. They tell us that the key strata of the planet should now move continuously to their normal positions and the intensity of the frequency barrier will diminish proportionately. The extraterrestrials have been observing earthquakes, volcanic eruptions and nuclear bomb detonations in order to monitor the diminishing frequency barrier. They tell us that when the barrier is gone, we will face new challenges and spiritual responsibilities.

A 14-page section in an Air Force Academy textbook states: "Extraterrestrials might have already tried to contact us on a different plane of awareness and we are not yet sensitive to communication on such a plane." It is evident by this statement that the U.S. government is aware of the existence of the frequency barrier and the visiting extraterrestrials and feel safe in saying, "UFOs are no threat to the security of the United States."

Giant Step

Hello to you on this road of life,
You seem to be going my way.
How hard has it been for you, my friend,
To walk this far today?
Rest your burden a little while
And sit beside me here.
Though a stranger I appear to you,
Please do not have fear.
The path that you and I must take
Is very much the same.
Wanting to meet you at this time of life,
Through galaxies of stars I came.
Your world is wakening from a deep, deep sleep;
Your thoughts are confused and new.
Our path is under a rainbow bridge –
May I walk with you?
Awake I've been for many a year;
I was up before the dawn.
I saw your world go to sleep
And watched its awakening yawn.
The rainbow bridge lies just ahead
Where your rockets soar through the sky.

Beyond that bridge there are men like you
And a man from there am I.
Rockets are not my way
But a silvery disk of light.
It matters not of these things,
For we're equal in God's sight.
Let us please go hand in hand
Across God's starry road.
Place your burden in my silvery disk;
It will carry your load.
Step by step we will go
On a journey far beyond Mars.
Let us take these steps together,
They'll be giant steps into the stars.

6

Vril Energy: the Psychic Charge Force

September 1991

Vril energy is the highest form of energy in the universe. All other forms of energy are actually lesser forms of this supreme force. It is the very creative force of God.

Every form of life must possess a minimum amount of this energy in order to live. The type of vril energy (in a slightly lower form) that maintains life will be hereafter referred to as "the charge force."

The charge force has been known or refered to as the life force, psychic force, internal fire and kundalini (to name but a few).

Experiencing Vril through Emotions

The individual human psyche can attract additional amounts of the charge force to it, and can likewise expend this precious energy. In fact, we as humans spend this energy by way of our emotions, such as hate, anger, fear, worry, envy, jealousy, desire, lust, the admiration of unworthy individuals, or the worship of false gods. We also expend this energy quite willingly (in most cases) through the emotional expressions of rightful appreciation, tenderness, fondness, compassion and love.

Humans give the psychic charge force to animals, and some animals reciprocate by returning the energy by way of their various expressions of love.

Acquiring Vril Honestly or Dishonestly

Humans can acquire the charge force from others in either an honest or dishonest fashion. Either form of acquisition is called a "charge vehicle." An honest type of charge vehicle brings its motivator charge not only from other people but also from the Supreme Creator (God Most High). An honest charge vehicle will not interfere with anyone or anything anywhere in the universe that is attempting to live and function in harmony with the Master Plan of the Supreme Creator.

A dishonest charge vehicle is one which is deliberately designed to disregard the basic human and spiritual rights of others. A person that deliberately employs a dishonest method for attracting and accumulating the charge force from others can rightfully be called a psychic vampire.

Using Art

A good example of a charge vehicle is seen when an artist such as a painter produces and maintains the proper mood and mental focus (mental discipline) that informs him or her when and where to apply their talent to the canvas. The mental focus cost the painter some amount of personal psychic charge force to maintain. If the finished painting does not offend the Master Plan of the Supreme Creator, charge energy in a greater amount than what was expended to create the painting is returned to the artist from the Supreme Source.

If the artist's painting is put on display and is in a position to be admired by others, any emotional response evoked by the painting in its viewers also provides additional charge energy for the artist. This form of charge force flow will continue to benefit the artist (embodied or disembodied) as long as the painting remains intact, and available for others to admire. *Any* form of charge vehicle is an act of "creation" (subcreation) even if the vehicle creates a "dark" (tormenting) emotional state in one or more persons.

Using Sex

Sex is both an act of creation and a communication in which large amounts of charge energy are exchanged willingly or sometimes unwillingly by the participants. Sometimes the charge flow during the act is one-sided. Unselfishness on the part of one or both participants brings a return of the psychic charge force from the Supreme Creator.

Renaissance artists such as Leonardo da Vinci and Michaelangelo painted religious themes that expressed clearly the fact that these artists somehow knew or intimately felt the source of the creative energy they so skillfully applied.

Walls of caves once occupied by primitive man depict both animals and hunting scenes. These cave paintings are some of the earliest forms of charge vehicles that still exist on Earth.

Sculpting in stone is one of mankind's most enduring types of charge vehicle, as such a vehicle requires the least maintenance or protection from the elements (or man-made pollution) to survive for a considerable period of time.

Using Dramatic, Musical and Sports Performance

Acting and singing publicly are other forms of charge vehicles. Actors will admit that they want to act on stage because they enjoy the emotional emissions from a live audience.

Daredevil-type stunts, patriotic displays (parades), rock concerts, and sporting events attract considerable amounts of charge force for their participants from those who observe them. Some people who are fanatically hooked on such things provide the psychic energy that perpetuates such activities. The term "fan" is short for "*fan*atic." Intense, continuous gambling is another form of charge vehicle that is most costly.

Restoration or repair of an object of art extends the charge vehicle to include and benefit the restorer(s) as well as the original artist. On the other hand, if a creative work of any type is deliberately marred or damaged, the *charge* energy spent by those saddened or angered by the event goes to the vandal. Such charge-hungry, attention-getting acts extend from being destructive up to even the false confession of a crime.

Incomplete creative works destroyed accidentally or on purpose by fire releases (frees) the creative energy into the universe, where by Divine Order the energy is returned to the vehicle's original creator.

When a women applies make-up and therefore enhances her beauty, she is actually making herself a more attractive charge vehicle.

Using Political Demogoguery

Adolph Hitler put a charge vehicle in motion to conquer the world and almost succeeded. His fiery speeches and programs of racial hate drew vast amounts of the psychic charge force from his fellows. When his people became disillusioned with him, his vehicle fell apart and he failed. When we recall Hitler's atrocities with bitter emotions, we cannot help but provide his soul more of the psychic charge force. Being human as we are, it is difficult, of course, not to feel emotional about the horrendous acts committed by a fellow man.

Jim Jones in Jonestown, Guyana had his approximatly 900 devotees drink cyanide, creating for him horrible memories that presently feed him charge wherever his eternal soul exists.

"Graven Images"

"Thou shalt have no other gods before me. Thou shalt not make unto thee any graven image, or any likeness of anything that is that is in heaven above, or that is in the earth beneath, or that is in the water under the earth" (Exodus 20:3,4). These statements are of course the first two of the Ten Commandments given by the "Lord God" to Moses on Mount Sinai. A graven image (or false god) such as a "Golden Calf" is the creation of an artisan or group of artisans who actually receive the charge force spend by those who worship their created idol. Fanatic, spiritually charged religious rituals encouraged by the priests of a false god, such as: human sacrifice also draws charge for the idol's creator(s) and its priests (the latter are actually extending, maintaining and perpetuating the vehicle).

The charge force that is given up during the worship of the Supreme Creator and other lesser but true spiritual entities is always returned to those who accept by faith their divine existence and purposes.

Stepped Down to ATP

The charge force is physically detectable when it is stepped down (transformed) into other types of energy. The force leaves the psychic part of our being (in amounts dictated by both physical and emotional demands) and resides (in all forms of animal life) in the molecule adenosine tri-phosphate (ATP). Upon receiving electrical signals from the brain, this molecule breaks apart and delivers the energy in an altered form, that in turn allows our muscles to perform.

When the human body is unable to produce enough ATP to step down the raw and powerful charge force to an acceptable level the body will ignite and burst into flames (spontaneous human combustion). Many cases of this phenomenon are on record. In most cases only the body is consumed. Articles around the remains are usually just scorched or slightly melted.

"Poltergeist" in German means "noisy ghost." Poltergeist activity amounts to the sudden event of objects (such as furniture) lifting into the air, flying about, and crashing into walls. In most documented cases there is in the vicinity a young person (usually female) who had recently reached the age of puberty. Here we have excessive amounts of ATP and other biochemicals in the young girl's body that are increasing the demand for charge force from her psyche. The increased and amplified charge in amounts beyond what the girl's physical body can tolerate, disperses in to her immediate environment, and becomes the motivating force that mysteriously causes the objects to fly about. Controlled use of the charge force to move objects is called "mind over matter" or telekinesis.

Seen in Kirlian Photographs

Dr. Thelma Moss, who once directed the Department of Parapsychology at the University of California at Los Angeles (UCLA) conducted studies that employed the Russian-invented photographic technique known as "Kirlian Photography." Kirlian photography applies electrical voltage to a photographic plate (usually Polaroid) in a manner that permits the image of any object touching the plate to be uniquely photographed. The resulting photographs show the object (animate or inanimate) surrounded by a halo of energy. Dr. Moss showed how the energy halo around the fingertips of sober people differed from persons who were intoxicated. Further more moving picture footage (exposed by the Kirlian technique) of a male and female kissing revealed the manifestation of a secondary energy spot at the point where the couples finger tips were touching on the plate. This spot grew both in size and intensity as the kiss progressed. These photographic experiments reveal the presence of the charge force in the energy halos (auras) of the subjects. The kiss experiment provides us with strong evidence that the charge force is indeed spent during a period of emotion.

Dr. Moss cut pieces off plant leaves and Kirlian-photographed them. The resulting photographs showed an energy outline (halo) that included the shape of the missing piece of the leaf. This is called the "phantom leaf effect."

The Energy Field of Objects

The energy around any inanimate object made by man represents the charge that was invested in the object's design and manufacture. Because of this *the charge force is the basis of the extraterrestrials' economic and monetary system.* The extraterrestrials are able to determine to the finest degree the amount of psychic charge force that was used in anything created by man. Because the charge force is a universal form of energy, it permits one type of extraterrestrial to trade with any other culture using the same system. Unlike an economic system based on an exhaustible precious metal supply or a slow-growing gross national product, the extraterrestrial economic system is growing exponentially minute by minute because the Supreme Creator returns greater amounts of charge force to anyone who created (acted as a subcreator) something beneficial to the Creator's Master Plan.

When a fire fly is looking for a mate it releases an amount of charged ATP into its abdomen, in which exists two chemicals, called ludiferin and luciferase. On contact the combined chemicals and ATP react, emitting a pulse of light. A device employing these chemicals along with Kirlian photography is presently being designed. The intensity of the emitted light will reveal the psychic energy value of the object in question, or the amount of charge force that is presently in the inventory of an individual.

Using For Teleportation & Telekinesis

An individual extraterrestrial's way of life employs the use of the charge force, in ways that exceed our imagination. For instance, they use the force to instantly communicate (telepathically) to each other over vast distances of space and to control the operation of their spacecraft by way of telekinesis.

The economic system of the extraterrestrials will be addressed in finer detail in a future article entitled "The Federation and the Trading Houses."

Beware: There are those of extraterrestrial origin who would like to keep us of the Earth ignorant of the existence of the charge force and of its importance and valuable uses. These "cosmic crooks" hope that we will foolishly give our psychic charge force to them, awed by their false superiority and advanced technology. Luckily, others from space have seen fit to tell us of the charge force and warn us about those who have it in mind to Vampire it from us.

CHARIOTS OF THE GODS

Thundering sounds in ancient skies,
Wise men with knowing nods,
Turn toward the heavens to behold
The Chariots of the Gods

From the stars they came
In those bygone days.
Then they came again and again.
To plant the seeds of knowledge
And thought in the minds of men.

Their marks are found on Nazca's plain,
And high on an Andes peak,
Their voices heard once again
Whenever the pyramids speak.

When men of earth go forth in space
And land on alien sod,
Strange eyes will behold their departure from
The Chariots of the Gods.

Wes Bateman

7

The Universal Life Field: Levels Of Perception

October 1991

Extraterrestrial sources tell us that all forms of life exist and have their being within an "omnipresent, all-permeating Universal Life Field" (ULF). Furthermore, when any of our physiological systems or organs lose any degree of harmony with the ULF we become susceptible to illness. If any of our biological systems lose total harmony with the ULF, we simply die.

The ULF is composed of a countless number of levels of perception, each pertaining to particular types of life function. Some of these functions (grouped under "extrasensory" or "psi phenomena") though commonplace to the extraterrestrials, still evade our earthly recognition and/or comprehension.

The meaning of extrasensory perception can be best understood by considering the following: To a person who is blind, those of us who can see have extrasensory perception, and the highest form of extrasensory perception would allow a person to perceive the will and purposes of the Supreme Creator. This highest form of perception is sometimes called cosmic consciousness or the ability to form the "infinite thought."

Though the ULF is composed of a countless number of levels, the extraterrestrials chose to divide it into four basic levels that have been named the *molar* level, *micro* level, *macro* level and *mega* level. These levels can be somewhat subdivided into what are called L-fields. Some L-fields have been physically recognized as relating to such things as biorhythms, female ovulation of humans and animals, and plant growth and reproduction. For further information regarding L-fields, I recommend the book *Life Fields* by Dr. Raymond Saxon Burr.

We are presently residing in the **molar level of perception.** In this level we employ five senses: seeing, hearing, smelling, tasting, and feeling by touching. The brain is both a molar-level translator of these senses and (on occasion, depending on conditions) a motivator of the senses "that is, encouraging the body to seek sensual stimulation.)

Though the brain is molar, the mind is not. The mind and its thoughts are of the **micro level of perception.** When a person dies, the psyche of an individual resides in the micro level of perception until embodiment into the molar level once again occurs. More will be said about the micro level of perception after the next level is described.

The macro level of perception is the realm of beings called the *Els.* The plural term for all the existing Els in the universe is *the Elohim.*

It was the Els who took the *el*ements (hydrogen, helium, lithium, etc.) and created the molar-level universe that we see about us. In other words, everything we see physically is the creative product of an El.

The name El is an ancient one, and it as a syllable has found its way into many of our languages. For instance, in English we find the syllable *el* in such words as: *el*der, elevate, int*el*lect, *el*ate, *el*ect, *el*ectric, *el*ite, and the devices of communication we call the t*el*ephone and t*el*evision (to name but a few).

The syllable *el* is found in the names of several Old Testament prophets: Ezeki*el*, *El*isha and Samu*el*. We also find the syllable *el* in the names of the seven Archangels: Ari*el*, Gabri*el*, Micha*el*, Uri*el*, Rapha*el*, Zadki*el*, and Jerim*el*. The word ang*el* itself means messenger of God.

There is an El (nature spirit) ruling over each and every planet in the universe. The extraterrestrials refer to an El as a "Lord God" and to the Supreme Creator as the "God Most High."

The Elohim know all there is to know about every reality that exists in the ULF. They never tire of t*el*ing or sp*el*ing out reality to each other. This continuous cosmic conversation is called the "song of the Els" or the "song of the spheres." The collective song of the Els gives us the name *uni-verse*, or one song.

The extraterrestrials symbolize an El as a one-eyed giant carrying a harp. The all-knowing, one-eyed Cyclops is the basis of the Greek word for the book of facts known as the en*cyclop*edia. The Els at the beginning of time disobeyed the Supreme Creator (violated the Master Plan) by prematurely creating the molar level of perception. An El's degree of participation in this violation caused its spirit to take on an identifying color, or hue. Thus there are red Els, green Els, blue Els and many shades between. We as humans (including all extraterrestrials) are products of the disobedient Els, and share our basic aura color with that of our parent El. For this reason we are called *hu*man or colored man. The Aztec god of nature in general was called Hu Mac Ku, the *mac* part of the name meaning the macro level of perception. The El's violation of the Master Plan of the Supreme Creator will be described further in a future article of this series.

The extraterrestrials tell us that we were all born of a particular El in the micro level of perception. At the time of our micro level birth we were nonpolarized entities (both male and female). In the micro level such an entity becomes divided into polarized psyches, representing one male and on some worlds as many as seven females. These male and female divisions are called "soul mates."

We take molar-level bodies in order to focus our psychic energy and perform deeds in this level that might be rewarded by the reacceptance and pardon of our parent El by the Supreme Creator. In other words, we are a part of a vast universal repair program.

We, as children of the Els, are benefited by the fact that we, as they, know everything there is to know about the Supreme Creator and the Universe. When we become aware of a reality or concept in the molar level, we actually bridge (by way of the brain) our micro-level knowledge of the subject to the molar-level facts concerning the subject. This process is called learning. When and if we bridge all we know in the micro level of perception, to the respective counterparts in the molar level of perception, we acquire the ability of *infinite thought*. The ability to infinitely think is also bestowed on a person who can relate even one micro-level reality *perfectly* to its molar-level equivalent, *as all is really one.*

The Els use the number 1.618033989 (phi or ϕ) to proportion everything they created. We as well as animals are proportioned on this number and its associated ratios derived from numbers known as Fibonacci numbers. (Fibonacci was an Italian mathematician of the Middle Ages.) The value of phi is the basis of the Fibonacci logarithmic spiral. This spiral is found in the shape of the ram's horn and the shell of the chambered nautilus and snail (to name a few). For more information on these number/nature relationships see my three-volume series, *The Rods of Amon Ra* (also published by Light Technology).

The **mega level of perception** is solely controlled by the Supreme Creator. An ancient name for the Creator is *Al.* As a syllable we find in it the words such as *al*l, v*al*ue, chemic*al*, re*al*ity, etc.. The term person*al*ity describes how we express (or do not express) the part of the Creator that is within us all.

The older the language, the purer it is. Is it not curious that the National Israeli Airline is called *El-Al?*

In the Book of Revelations the Supreme Creator is referred to as "Alpha and Omega, the beginning and the end." Alpha and omega are, respectively, the first and last letters in the Greek alphabet. Letters make up words and words describe re*al*ity, and the Supreme Creator is all forms of reality. Letters *let* and describe reality, but numbers also describe reality in a *numb*ing or fixating way.

Whereas phi is the number of the Els, (pi $\pi = 3.1415926+$) is the Creator's number. Pi is both irrational (can't be written as a fraction) and transcendental (beyond the range of the senses). Pi appears to amount to a string of numbers that continue to some point in infinity (or forever). Pi is, of course, known as the ration that exists between a circle's diameter and its circumference.

The human brain produces four distinct brain-wave patterns. They have been assigned names of Greek letters: delta, theta, alpha and beta. We generate delta and theta waves when we are asleep. We generate alpha brain waves when in astate of relaxed meditation. Beta waves are generated when we are aware of the world around us.

Alpha waves range from 7 to 13.5 Hz (cycles per standard second). Alpha waves of 10.6 Hz occur most frequently.

When the deepest average alpha wave of 10.6 is divided by the last alpha-wave frequency of 13.5 Hz, the result is .7851851851 (close to 1/4 the value of Pi). Other data suggest that the deepest alpha-wave frequency average is 10.602875 Hz per *natural second.* Thus this value, divided by 13.5 Hz (per natural second) equals .78539814814 (1/4 pi).

The information above suggests that we of the earth use about 1/4 the value of pi in our thinking processes, and when one of us gains the ability to perceive the will of the Creator (infinite thought), their brain will operate on the full and most complete infinite value of pi.

We are proportioned on the order of phi (number of the Els) and think on the order of pi (Supreme Creator's number). Animals are proportioned by phi but do not use pi in their thought processes. The pi factor allows us to think int*el*igently. "Know ye not that ye are gods?"

8
The Forces Of Light And Darkness

It was explained in a previous article that we and all extraterrestrials exist within a Universal Life Field that the extraterrestrials divide into four major levels of perception. These levels are called the *molar* (physical) level, *micro* (mind/thought) level, *macro* (parent El) level and *mega* (Supreme Creator) level (see October issue of the *Sedona Journal for the Golden Age*).

We as humans (hue-man, or colored man) leave the consciousness of our parent El (who resides at the macro level of perception) and enter into the micro level of perception as a nonpolaric entity (no sexual identification). Once in the micro level such an entity divides into one male and one to seven females (depending on the particular molar-level reproduction purpose of the parent El). These divisions are called soulmates.

At different points in time the soulmates embody in the molar level. Into this lower level the male and female psyches have carried with them the desire to reunite into the nonpolaric entity state they experienced in the micro level. This desire is represented in the molar level by the sexual urge that ensures the El that physical reproduction will occur.

Once embodied in the molar level of perception, the psyche is able to attract, spend, focus and generally utilize its psychic energy (charge force) to subcreate on behalf of its El and the Supreme Creator (see September issue of *Sedona Calendar of Creative Happenings*).

In addition, the psyche brought with it into the molar level all the knowledge of its parent El. When the psyche comes into contact with and recognizes the molar-level representation of a reality or concept, we say that the person has learned. This bridging of macro to molar knowledge, or molar-level comprehension, is stored in the micro consciousness (mind) of the psyche as memory. If a person is able to "molarize" all knowledge or comprehend one molar reality or concept perfectly, that person will reach the highest level of extrasensory perception, which is to perceive the will of the Supreme Creator. Such an accomplishment (called the Infinite Thought) frees the psyche from any future obligation to its parent El (see October issue).

Once a person has achieved the ability of Infinite Thought (cosmic consciousness), that person has two choices: (1) being absorbed into the consciousness of the Supreme Creator, thus becoming one and the same; or (2) remaining in the molar level as spiritual guides for those not yet reperfected. Such individuals can be called Angels. There are two types of persons that have had the Infinite Thought: (1) those who have included the complex spiritual nature of mankind in their formulation of the Infinite Thought ("Noble Infinite Thought") and (2) those whose ability to form the Infinite Thought was based on the study of one thing or all things not pertaining to the spiritual nature of mankind. The latter type of individual (Master) continues to pursue the Noble Infinite Thought by taking on the role of teacher, where they teach themselves.

Neither type of individual capable of the Infinite Thought can pass it on to another, as any receiver would have to have full molar-level knowledge to comprehend it. Therefore the Infinite Thought is the one thing each must attain for him/herself.

A reperfected person will *not in any way interfere with or direct* the lives of anyone not yet reperfected, but will provide a person (if asked) with "Lights of Divine Direction."

If a person asks one who is perfect if she/he should take a particular action, the Angel or true Master will inquire of the Supreme Consciousness if the proposed action is in harmony with the Creator's Master Plan. If it is in harmony, the perfect one receives consciously a White Light, indicating that the proposed action will not interfere with anything anywhere in the universe that is also functioning in harmony with the Master Plan. If no light is received, the meaning is to the contrary. A grey light means that only the person originating the inquiry will lose (temporarily or permanently) the harmonious relationship they presently have with the Master Plan.

When the extraterrestrials are asked why they do not land on the White House lawn or contact the leaders of the world or physically deal with the inhabitants of the Earth, they simply reply, "We have received no White Light permitting us to do so."

Destiny

As explained earlier, when we leave the micro level of perception and embody in the molar level, we do so as male or female. But some psyches leave the micro level possessing more or less psychic pressure than their immediate spiritual relatives (those originating from the same El). An individual's psychic pressure does influence his/her higher performance in the molar level. Those with relatively large psychic pressures are somewhat hindered because they require more psychic energy to function, but they generally have the mental ability to comprehend the total picture or plan of something. Persons with relatively lower psychic pressures usually become specialists in one occupation or another. *Psychic pressure is in no way to be considered a spiritual caste system, as a person's level of pressure does not affect his/her intelligence or spirituality.*

In our first molar-level lives as "hue-mans" we establish a psychic character that we will represent life after life unless we make a conscientious effort during the course of a physical lifetime to change that character for the better (or worse). This means that life after life we are dealt the same cards; the difference is in how we play them. We establish this repetitious pattern ("destiny pattern") in our first human life by committing more than half of our psychic (emotional) energy to someone or something. These events establish what are called "destiny points." (The difference between destiny, karma and their relationship to psychic pressure will be the subject of a future article.)

Life after life we encounter destiny points, though not necessarily in the order they were established in the first life. Sometimes they are preceded by a feeling that the person had been at a place, event or had met someone before (*deja vu*).

Let us imagine that a person's first life as a human was being a thief. That person will carry within their aura the symbolic distortion that represents a thief. If in a life that follows, an opportunity to steal arises but the person refrains from stealing, the destiny distortion disappears from the person's aura and remains absent unless the person once again commits a theft. This illustrates the meaning of the passage in the Lord's Prayer that says, "Lead us not into temptation."

At the time a mob was about to stone a woman to death for adultery, Jesus Christ knelt before the crowd and wrote in the sand "robber, adulterer, blasphemer." The Christ was actually reading the destiny distortions in the auras of the woman's accusers. Jesus also said, "Ye who are without sin cast the first stone."

There are both good destiny points and destiny points that are uncomfortable to live with. But once each and every destiny point is encountered and favorably handled in one lifetime, all symbols disappear from the individual's aura and the basic aura color of the person changes. Eventually in one lifetime or another the individual's basic aura color will be black. Black contains all colors and represents *the highest form of material perfection*. The color white, on the other hand, also contains all colors, but represents *the highest form of spiritual perfection* (aura color of a reperfected person). The difference between the colors white and black can only be understood by a person who has had the Infinite Thought.

The extraterrestrials do not refer to the color black as being evil, but they refer to those who deliberately practice evil as the "forces of darkness," darkness meaning the absence of light. They also say, "The light from the stars requires a field of blackness to enhance their presence and their magnificence."

The extraterrestrials make every effort not to become too emotionally involved with a "firstborn" person to avoid becoming eternally attached to that person's destiny pattern in the making. Firstborns are easily recognized by personality traits that show them to be childlike, naive and somewhat gullible.

In extraterrestrial cultures, firstborns are kindly nurtured and protected; on the other hand, they do take advantage of emotional relationships (destinies) that are already established between individuals. This practice will be explained shortly.

The Two Sides of the Wheel

In the universe there exist those who desire to have the power of the Creator without following the Creator's Master Plan or attaining the Infinite Thought. These individuals collectively compose the "forces of darkness," who encourage and conduct warfare against those who wish to live peacefully within the Creator's Master Plan. They are constantly devising ways to spiritually control others and psychically vampire their psychic energy. (Some of the ways the evil ones use to obtain the power of the Creator while still remaining imperfect will be the subject of a future article.)

The extraterrestrials refer to those who follow the Master Plan or those that practice evil as "opponents on the wheel of life." The extraterrestrials state that they can physically keep score of who is winning the battle for psychic control of the universe. The side that is presently winning (but not victorious) would be the side that has control of the most psychic energy in the form of objects (weapons) or humans dedicated to their particular cause.

The evil side of the wheel takes advantage of an individual's destiny points in order to psychically enslave and steal their psychic energy life after life. In other words, they prevent some people from shedding their detrimental destiny points and thus keep them from progressing in the Creator's Master Plan, for such a progression eventually moves their victim out of their control.

As said earlier, even those who work within the Master Plan of the Creator take advantage of emotional relationships (destinies) that are already established between individuals. They form groups that they know will get together in every life due to their respective destinies. Then they arrange for those groups to be physically born on a planet such as the Earth. It is the extraterrestrials' hope that these individuals and groups will assemble because of their destiny relationships and work together for the good of universal mankind. Such a prearranged assemblage of psyches is called a Patrax.

At one time in the distant past it was asked of those who have had the Infinite Thought whether those who are psychic slaves to the other side of the wheel will ever be free to function in the Creator's Master Plan and be able to pursue the Infinite Thought. By Lights of Divine Direction and the process of elimination it was realized that a New Reality would come forth that will free all people from evil psychic enslavement. Furthermore, it was realized that this New Reality would manifest in the "frequency barrier" of planet Earth (for information on the frequency barrier, see the August 1991 issue of *Sedona Calendar of Creative Happenings*).

Upon hearing about the forthcoming New Reality, the extraterrestrials put together a Patrax for planet Earth that they hope will support the manifestation of this New Reality. Time after time Patrax groups embodied on Earth only to disband without coming in contact with any sort of New Reality. As time grew close, Lights of Divine Direction once again provided information that the New Reality would manifest in the form of a man. Ever since the birth of that man, the extraterrestrials of good intent have made every effort not to disrupt the full manifestation of that reality. The life, death and resurrection of that exceptional man collectively represent the New Reality. The man was, of course, Jesus. The reality is reverently referred to by most extraterrestrials as the Christ Reality. The subject of the Christ Reality will be covered in next month's Christmas issue of *Sedona Journal for the Golden Age.*

There exist numerous extraterrestrial Patrax groups presently living on Earth who are prepared to support the full manifestation of the Christ Reality. Maybe you, the reader, are destined to psychically awake and recall a Plan you became part of a long time ago on some faraway world your soul calls home.

9

Dulce: How Sweet Is It?

February 1992

The geographical location where the borders of Arizona, New Mexico, Utah and Colorado meet is called the "Corners." Located close to the meeting point of these four borders is the town of Dulce, New Mexico. Dulce is the Spanish word for sweet.

For several years rumors have circulated about the existence of an underground extraterrestrial biological laboratory located in the desert near the town of Dulce. In addition, stories are told and published again and again that describe aliens conducting horrible biological experiments on abducted earthlings at their Dulce base. The stories all say that the aliens' purpose in conducting these experiments is to produce biological monstrosities. That is, to combine a number of various life forms into one, i.e. part dog/part human, or part horse/part human.

I have been asked many times to comment on these stories and have been somewhat reluctant, due to the fact that my data might contribute to the fear the Dulce stories induce in most people. I have given in to the many requests to publish what I have learned about the alien Dulce base, not to intentionally instill more fear, but to focus on its original purpose, history, and its present status. It is my hope that this article will clear the air and refocus our attention on the real past, present or future dangers that might stem from the presence of the ET lab at Dulce.

The construction of the underground laboratory at Dulce was begun by a certain group of extraterrestrials in the early 1920s. This secret project was not fully operational until about 1938. The extraterrestrial builders and operators of the lab intended to keep its presence secret from all but a few earthlings.

Those of the Earth in the know about the Dulce base were certain high officials of the German Nazi party. The Dulce ETs encouraged the Nazis in their belief in a super-race and the annihilation of those races the extraterrestrials declared inferior. The Dulce ETs could not take any chances on the outcome of World War II, nor did they want to assist the Nazis in a way that would reveal their presence on the Earth and thus bring the wrath of other opposing extraterrestrials down on their heads. That is, if the Nazis did *not* win the war, their base at Dulce would remain secret, would still be operational and not subject to any form of attack by those extraterrestrials that opposed its diabolical purpose.

During WWII the Dulce base was fully stocked by concentration camp prisoners provided by their Nazi allies. As the war was coming to an end in Europe, the Dulce ETs attempted to assist the Nazis technically by providing them with the specifications for jet engines and a "flying disc." This assistance came too late. The Nazis did produce jet aircraft but were not able to build enough of them to reverse their eventual downfall. The Nazi flying disc program was carried out in the Cordovan mountain range of Argentina. Two discs were completed, but not until the war had been over for several years. These discs were destroyed when they crashed in the early 1950s in Sweden and South Africa, respectively.

Near the end of the war the Federation ETs, who opposed the Dulce ETs, began to escort Allied bombers to and from their targets in Germany in order to discourage any form of physical attack by the malevolent ETs. German pilots thought that the escorting disc-shaped craft belonged to the Allies and the Allied pilots thought the discs were German.

The discs were nicknamed "foo-fighters" after the statement repeatedly made by comic strip fireman Smokey Stover, "Where there's smoke there's foo."

After the end of WWII several notable UFO incidents took place. One incident in particular was obviously a hostile ET action. This incident resulted in the disappearance of five Torpedo bombers (Flight 19), a Martin Mariner, and a Navy Privateer in December 1945 off the coast of Florida (see the June 1991 issue).

The subject of UFOs became public knowledge in June 1947 when Kenneth Arnold reported to the press that he had observed from his private plane a fleet of nine disc-shaped aircraft flying in formation near Mt. Rainier in the state of Washington.

For the remainder of the decade and into the early 1950s UFO reports were abundant. The U.S. Air Force did its best to debunk as many sighting reports as it could. Its motto at the time seemed to be, "If you can't wow them with wisdom, baffle them with baloney."

For a period after the Arnold sighting inhabitants of the Southwestern part of the U.S – especially around the Four Corners area – were to witness a rash of green fire balls shooting across the skies. This phenomenon continued for several years and then stopped just as suddenly as it began.

During the time of the green fireball activity (July 1947), a UFO was found crashed in the desert near Roswell, New Mexico. It is reported that a number of alien bodies were recovered from this wreck. Autopsies showed that the aliens had no digestive systems and a search of the downed craft did not uncover any sign of foodstuffs or any other form of provisions. In addition, these creatures had no apparent sexual organs nor was it possible to determine how they were able to reproduce. The earliest U.S. government conclusions was that these creatures were *genetically engineered mutants* (most likely clones of one original individual).

There is an account of a surviving alien who was named "Ebe" (Extraterrestrial Biological Entity), who wasted away after a short period of captivity.

There are also reports of UFO wreckage being found at the same time in all of the Four Corner states and in northern Mexico. These wrecked spacecraft were definite evidence that warfare was under way between two or more extraterrestrial groups.

What does it all mean? What did these events have to do with the alien Dulce base? In order to answer these two questions, we must answer several other questions first.

Why would any extraterrestrial (or anyone, for that matter) want to produce biological monstrosities?

Nature has natural biological barriers that prevent interspecie mating. A mule is the offspring of a horse and a donkey, but cannot reproduce. The extraterrestrials are aware that successful biological (genetic) engineering able to produce a pair of mutants that in turn could reproduce would bestow the powers of godhood on those creating this new species. This, then, was the extraterrestrial purpose for establishing the Dulce base.

With all the numerous planets that exist in the universe, why have the extraterrestrials chosen the Earth to conduct these secret experiments? Why not take the biological subjects or material to their native worlds and conduct their experiments unhindered?

The reason the Dulce ETs selected the Earth for the site of their experimental laboratory is simple. The Earth provides a powerful ingredient for biological mutation not found anywhere else in the universe. This ingredient for controlled mutation is in the form of the *frequency barrier* (see the August 1991 issue). It was explained in the May 1991 issue that the creatures known as *Sasquatch* (Bigfoot) were also part of hostile ET biological experiments being conducted within the frequency barrier of the planet Earth.

It is also noteworthy to recall that the same type of hostile ETs were working in the field of biological mutation even before the frequency barrier began on the Earth. They made attempts to combine the physical forms of humans and animals using the power that naturally accumulates and focuses in pyramids, which were designed with sacred geometry. From these attempts, learned from legend, the ancient Egyptians derived the forms of their gods, such as the Sphinx, which is half man and half lion.

Why would any other type of extraterrestrial bother to stop such experiments?

The answer is now quite obvious. If the hostile ETs gain the power of godhood from the success of their evil experiments, that power could be used to subject and enslave any and all cultures that exist throughout the universe.

The Overview

For thousands of years the extraterrestrials that compose the Federation were content to observe the geological changes causing the diminishment of the frequency barrier on the Earth. There was no reason to establish and maintain bases in the harsh environment of the barrier. Even though they had the technology to construct barrier-free havens (bases) on the planet, the Federation chose to let the frequency barrier run its course, no matter how long it took.

The hostile ETs had to keep within the frequency-barrier-free environment of their base or transport spacecraft. This was quite limiting for them. They suffered these restrictions during WWII but knew that without Nazi help they had to take bolder action in order to operate worldwide.

They thought they might solve their problem by using a mutant strain of beings that they developed off the Earth. These mutants were developed to function in the frequency barrier as we do, and were trained in many ways to serve their masters. The extraterrestrials call these mutants "Corts." We know them as the "Greys" and "Long-Nose Greys." The U.S. Government calls them Extraterrestrial Biological Entities (EBEs).

The hostile ETs kept their Corts obedient and under control by the fact that they had no digestive tracts and relied on a special intravenous diet to live – and of course, this nutrient could only be provided by their masters. The lack of this nutrient caused the Corts to waste away and die.

In desperation, the Dulce ETs ordered a contingent of Corts sent to the Earth starting in 1947. Their arrival was the reason for the rash of UFO sightings reported at the time.

After learning of the existence of the Dulce base and the influx of Corts having the Dulce base as their destination, the Federation was forced to take action in the form of shooting down the spacecraft of the incoming Corts. The destruction of these spacecraft resulted in the reported green fireballs. One of the components in the propulsion systems of the downed spacecraft contained vast amounts of the element thallium (atomic number 81). The most prominent spectral line of thallium is brilliant green. Seeing this green line in his spectroscope for the first time, the discoverer of thallium named this element after the Greek name for the color of a budding twig. Because the incoming Cort spacecraft had the Dulce base as a destination, most of the debris from the shattered craft fell within the general Four Corners area and northern Mexico. The Aztec, New Mexico, UFO wreckage mentioned earlier was found less than fifty miles from the town of Dulce.

This extraterrestrial warfare was also witnessed in Australia. Witnesses reported seeing one UFO shoot another out of the sky. Within the last two years, a supermarket tabloid reported that in the early 1950s inhabitants of an entire African village witnessed UFO dogfights that resulted in the destruction of some of the participants.

Worldwide reports of ET warfare and the scattered remains of the crashed vehicles concentrated throughout the Four Corners area brought the presence of the Dulce ET base to the attention of the U.S. Government. By the time of the Eisenhower administration, the U.S. Government thought they were ready to take action against the Dulce base. Prior to this action, surviving Corts representing the Dulce ETs met with President Eisenhower at Modoc Air Force Base in California. Their masters set up this meeting to strike a deal. Their proposal was to trade high technology for the right to continue operating their base at Dulce. Eisenhower wisely put them off until he could communicate with the other side of the extraterrestrial conflict.

Another Modoc meeting took place at which Federation representatives spoke from within the barrier-free environment of their spacecraft to General Curtis LeMay, who, in turn, spoke for President Eisenhower. The Federation representatives were obviously two different types of humans. Because of their blond and red hair, they were referred to respectively as the "Nordic" and the "Orange." During this meeting a fleet of UFOs numbering in the thousands took up orbit around the Earth's equator and departed at the completion of the talks. The downside of the talks was that the Federation was not willing to give high technology *only* to the United States and told LeMay not to expect anything of real value from the Dulce ETs. In essence, they said, those of Dulce were setting up a con.

The U.S. Government decided not to trust either side and planned to militarily storm the Dulce base. The Federation advised against such action and pleaded for time to negotiate directly with the extraterrestrials in control of the base. The Federation then advised the occupants of the Dulce base to pack up and leave the Earth under a flag of truce. Knowing that the Federation had them "bottled up" and that they could not get any supplies through the Federation blockade, they agreed to depart. The Dulce ETs hermetically sealed the base and departed, leaving their experiments and biological cultures still active within.

The Federation then asked the U.S. Government to allow them to open the Dulce base and safely remove its vile contents. The Government refused, believing that the Federation only wanted to profit from the work of their departed enemy.

An unknown number of men with varied specialties began to penetrate the Dulce base. They were met by very advanced booby traps. At some time in the 1950s they succeeded in achieving total access to the base. It is reported that this operation cost about 300 lives.

At the time of final penetration, the excavators were met by a tremendous blast of heat and "pocket explosions" that took place on various levels of the underground complex. As a consequence, biological agents heretofore never part of Earth's biological or ecological system were released into the planet's biosphere. There were no apparent, immediate effects or danger realized by the U.S. Government as it began to study the remains of alien technology that had come under their control.

The Dulce base had been equipped with a mixture of gases that collectively produce what is called a *rad* atmosphere. Such an atmosphere is easily breathed by any form of life. Even fish out of water can breathe it quite well. But when the rad gas mixture came in contact with the air of the Earth, it chemically reacted. This was the reason excavators reported the blast of heat and why the explosions took place within the base at the time of final penetration.

The Federation warned that there was biological contamination not detectible by any means available to Earth science. They then requested that they be allowed to "clean up" the immediate environment. Not wishing to take any further chances, the government agreed to the ET clean-up project. The Federation recovered as much contamination as was possible and projected the waste into the sun.

The U.S. Government went further by hiring contractors to skim off a layer of surface soil and sink square-shaped shafts into the ground. It is reported by those who worked on digging the shafts that they were later lined with white tiles. It is also reported that the removed layer of soil was taken to ground zero locations where nuclear bombs were being tested. Even as late as 1968 the government was still disposing of biologically contaminated equipment and materials removed from the Dulce base. Under cover of a nuclear experiment, this material was disintegrated underground at Farmington, New Mexico. Farmington is located a little more than 100 miles west of Dulce. The government called the cover project "Gas Buggy" and pretended the nuclear detonation was to expose a natural gas deposit in the area. Anyone for radioactive natural gas? How did the government expect to keep the natural gas from catching fire from the heat of the nuclear explosion?

The U.S. Government then provided the Federation with a telephone line (located in a remote part of the Rocky Mountains) which they could tap into and call Washington at will.

The Aftermath

As time went on a number of strange things began to happen in the vicinity of the Four Corners area. The first being the mysterious death of flocks of sheep, in Utah. Enraged ranchers demanded an explanation from the government. After hemming and hawing, the government paid for the sheep stating that the deaths were a result of poison gas accidentally released into the wind from the Rocky Mountain arsenal. This story is untrue. These animals were actually victims of biological agents that were released from the Dulce ET base several years before.

In 1965 the strange story of "Snippy" the horse came to light. Near the town of Durango, Colorado, a rancher found the remains of one of her horses lying in a remote pasture. The horse had been totally drained of its blood and various organs had been surgically removed by someone with exceptional skill and expertise. There was no blood around the carcass, no footprints of man or predator, nor any physical evidence that might have shed some light on who could have performed the surgery on the animal. Durango, Colorado, is located (as the crow flies) about 75 miles northwest of Dulce.

Following the Snippy incident, cattle subjected to the same mysterious type of surgical procedures became commonplace in the Four Corners area. The mutilations, as they came to be called, then spread to the point where they are now reported worldwide.

The extraterrestrials of the Federation admit that they are humanely putting selective animals to death in order to acquire biological material and data that pertains to types of infection not yet detectible by earth science. They call this form of biological infection a "Jess." A Jess is a genetically engineered biological product that was produced to bridge the barriers that exist between the various animal species. The Jess temporarily suspends a person's imune system and allows for animal parts to be grafted to humans and not biologically rejected. The particular Jess the extraterrestrials are interested in relates to human biology. They tell us this product was released into the environment when the Dulce base was carelessly unsealed.

The bovine (cattle) species has a similar chromosome makeup to humans. Therefore, the Jess product found a compatible place to reside and continued to mutate in the frequency barrier environment. Because the product mutates slowly over a period of years, new biological data acquired from certain types of cattle must be obtained. Therefore, we should expect to hear of more cattle mutilations.

Before the danger was realized by the governments of Earth, several things occurred. The Jess was passed onto cattle in other parts of the world by way of artificial insemination, a practice employed by cattle breeders to improve their stock. The second mistake was in using the blood products of horses and cows to produce medical vaccines.

In 1977 the World Health Organization (WHO) inoculated thousands of Africans against smallpox. As a result, the alien-produced Jess entered into the human population. Once established, the Jess in the human biological environment went about producing a virus that would, in controlled conditions, prevent the rejection of foreign biological tissue. In other words, it would have temporarily suspended the function of the body's immune system. In its rampant, increasingly mutating state the Jess-produced virus simply destroys a person's immune system. The term we give this biologically devastating condition is "acquired immune deficiency syndrome" (AIDS).

We can trace the spread of AIDS very easily. During the period when the WHO was inoculating Africans against smallpox, they also provided the vaccine to a large number of Haitians working on the continent at the time. These workers brought the disease back to Haiti, where the largest number of AIDS cases were first reported. The next place the disease emerged in large numbers was in South America. Most South American countries buy blood products from Africa.

In addition, inoculations against hepatitis were given in San Francisco, California, bringing about the same results as the vaccine given to the Africans against smallpox by the WHO.

The extraterrestrials state that AIDS is an individual disease. It mutates in relation to a person's individual biological makeup. A general vaccine against the disease is therefore difficult to formulate. The presence of the frequency barrier and its contribution to the further mutation of the Jess factor only adds to the difficulty.

By studying the Jess mutation rate in cattle, the extraterrestrials of the Federation are attempting to discover if the Jess will mutate itself out of existence or into a state of harmlessness. Furthermore, they are attempting to anticipate whether the frequency barrier will permit a general AIDS vaccine or cure with a formulation that will work for a period of time. When and if such a frequency barrier condition comes about, the new vaccine or cure should be administered. The frequency barrier is bound to change, so any unused vaccine of this type would become useless. Any change will, of course, require a reformulation of an AIDS vaccine or medical cure to one that would have a value at some future point in the ever-changing frequency barrier. The extraterrestrials would prefer to produce a medical cure for the disease – not a vaccine – because they do not wish to raise any suspicions (due to mistrust) about the Earth's population being vaccinated with a substance that was formulated in an extraterrestrial laboratory. Furthermore, they realize that the urgency to take such a vaccine within a short period of time might be construed as contrived psychological pressure, thereby raising unwarranted suspicions.

In essence, the extraterrestrials of the Federation are saying, "Hang in there, friends. We're working on it!"

10

Extraterrestrials: Now You See Them, Now You Don't

March 1992

The extraterrestrials tell us that *we as well as they* live within the confines of an "omnipresent all-permeating Universal Life Field" (U.L.F.).

There are a countless number of dimensions, or levels of awareness, that compose the U.L.F., but the ETs prefer to organize the field into four parts they call the **molar, micro, macro** and **mega** levels. Each succeeding level requires a greater degree of awareness in order to perceive or comprehend.

We on Earth live within the molar level of perception, in which we employ the five senses: seeing, hearing, smelling, tasting and feeling by touch. Because we deal with things that have the three dimensions of height, width and depth and the physical laws that pertain to them, we often refer to the molar level as the third dimension.

The extraterrestrials I communicate with live in the third dimension and require food, water and medical care, as we do. They also require three-dimensional forms of transportation to move them from one point in the universe to another. They have the technology to temporarily circumvent the physical laws of the molar level and engage physical laws that apply to higher levels of the U.L.F. In this manner they easily overcome the vast distances that exist between galaxies in three-dimensional space (see my book *Dragons and Chariots*).

When it comes to the third-dimensional (molar) level the extraterrestrials tell us we are being short-changed because there is much more to this level than we are able to perceive and therefore comprehend. Our vision is restricted to the narrow spectrum between infrared and ultraviolet, requiring instruments to view these two or any other wavelength of light that exists beyond either end of our visual spectrum. Most extraterrestrials are able to perceive with their naked eye far beyond the wavelengths of infrared or ultraviolet.

When we look at a blade of grass we say it is green in color, but it is actually every color *except* green. All the colors of the spectrum except one or more wavelengths of the color green are absorbed by the substances that compose the blade. In other words, only particular wavelengths of green are reflected to our eye and processed by our brain. Consequently, maybe only one of the several wavelengths of the reflected color is able to be processed by us mentally. The third-dimensional perception and mental processing abilities of the extraterrestrials is far beyond ours, for they are able to see all other wavelengths of color that might be reflected by the blade of grass. That is, they are able to see and therefore comprehend more of the third dimension than we are.

The extraterrestrials' abilities to hear, smell, taste and feel by touching is as superior as their ability to see. The extraterrestrials tell us that we too would have these increased abilities to perceive and process the realities of the third dimension (molar level) if we were not subjected to the detrimental effects of the frequency barrier (see article with this title in the August 1991 issue).

Some extraterrestrials would seem to be invisible to us, but do not appear so to anyone that has *full* third-dimensional perception. This phenomenon of invisibility relates to what is called "molecular frequency" and "mental scan rate." A person that has full third-dimensional perception has a higher (faster) mental scan rate.

If you were to take a picture of an operating television screen with a very fast shutter setting, the resulting picture would show only that portion of the TV picture that was projected to the inner face of the TV tube during the time of the film exposure. The longer the exposure, the more of the TV picture that will be on the film. The scan rate of the electron beam that projects the various numbers of TV picture lines on the inner face of the picture tube is timed to coincide with our mental scan rate. In synchronization with our scan rate, the picture appears to us to be solid (although it really isn't).

The molecules that compose the physical (third-dimensional) bodies of some extraterrestrial races are vibrating at frequencies that are beyond our present mental scan rate. To use the analogy of the TV picture, the picture lines would be projected so fast that the screen would always look blank to us.

Another analogy would be a fan blade rotating at a very high speed. The blade appears to be almost invisible, but touching the blade will prove without further doubt that it is a third-dimensional solid. In a nutshell, even extraterrestrials we cannot see are subjects of the third dimension (molar level of perception).

The higher an extraterrestrial's molecular frequency, the less they are physically able to tolerate the frequency barrier of planet Earth. Higher molecular frequencies are not to be misconstrued as being related to higher spirituality. They are strictly related to planetary origin. If we of the Earth lived in a frequency-barrier-free environment, all extraterrestrials would be visible to us.

Extraterrestrials of molecular-body frequencies as close to ours as possible generally carry out the ET program of observing geologically related frequency-barrier events on our planet. Even so, they must take extreme precautions to maintain a barrier-free environment within their vehicles.

From my personal experience, when a group of about 20 persons viewed and photographed an extraterrestrial spacecraft at night with infrared film, two of the group (men) were unable to see the craft hovering only several hundred feet away. The craft was invisible to the men because the wavelengths of light emitted from the craft could not be mentally processed by them. This phenomenon has been linked to the fact that both men were also color-blind. The resulting infrared photographs of the craft revealed it perfectly. Additional pictures taken with highly sensitive night film depicted, when developed, nothing but swirls of color resembling a child's finger painting.

Extraterrestrial spacecraft on many occasions appear to suddenly disappear before the eyes of observers. This phenomenon is based on one of three factors: (1) The ship simply accelerated instantly to light speed. (2) The magnetic field surrounding the craft was increased to such a strength that the light behind the craft was "bent" around it, giving the observer a view of the sky behind the vehicle (like the Romulan cloaking device on Star Trek). Sometimes the bending of light in this manner makes the craft appear to change shape (although it doesn't) due to shadows produced by the process. (3) The craft activated an inter-dimensional propulsion system that employs physical laws not regulated by the third dimension.

So what are these fourth-dimensional beings we keep hearing about? You might be surprised that you too are using fourth-dimensional abilities every time you think. But once again the extraterrestrials are able to use their fourth-dimensional (micro level) abilities to a greater degree than we are. In this area we are slowly catching up to them as the frequency barrier becomes less detrimental. Full fourth-dimension perception and awareness come with the ability to command all of the psi phenomena – such things as telepathy, telekinesis (mind over matter), spiritual healing etc. After death our micro level being resides in the fourth dimension until reembodiment. Therefore there are fourth-dimensional beings, but sooner or later they will reembody once again into the third dimension.

The macro level of perception is the realm of the Elohim. Even extraterrestrials wish to attain awareness in this level of perception, for to do so would bond them mentally once again to the parent El from which they originated.

Anyone attaining the mental ability to reach the macro level of perception will thereafter bear a golden ring within their aura, hear the song of the Els (song of the spheres), and be capable of performing miraculous things with the *el*ements of the third dimension such as turning water into wine.

To attain the mega level of perception is to attain the highest state of awareness, or, one might also say, the highest form of extrasensory perception. This is achieved either when an individual fully understands *every* reality in the universe perfectly or understands *one* reality perfectly. For all is really one.

A person who has attained awareness in the mega level of perception is said to have joined consciousness with the Creator of All That Is. This is called having the ability of Infinite Thought, or reaching the state of

Cosmic Consciousness.

At the time a person has the Infinite Thought they have the choice of being absorbed back into the consciousness of the Creator or remaining in a state from which they can physically function in the lower dimensions.

Those who choose the latter might appear suddenly before one's eyes and fade in and out of view many times within seconds. These reperfected persons play very important parts in the lives of the extraterrestrials (as explained in a previous article). But even to an extraterrestrial with full third- and fourth-dimensional awareness, at times they cannot mentally scan the vibration of the reperfected ones, and they therefore say, as we must about some of *them*, "Now you see them, now you don't."

11
I Am Darafina

May 1992

Assisted by Deanna Bateman

I have often been asked: "How did you ever come to be in contact with extraterrestrials?" This question is sometimes followed with descriptions of personal feelings of the inquirer, which are related to what seems to them to be a possible attempt by extraterrestrials to contact them. After revealing their suspicions, the inquirer generally asks: "How do I know it's really happening to me, and that I'm not going insane?"

Because of this type of interest, I have chosen to write of my own experience in order to possibly help those who might be opening up mentally (due to Frequency Barrier diminishment) to the point where mental contacts with extraterrestrials or some other form of psi ability may be naturally developing. Hopefully, this information will help overcome the strange confusion that might erroneously cause a person to seek treatment for a mental disorder from someone not familiar with the effects of such a mental transition. Misdiagnosis could have terrible consequences.

Some thirty years ago (1961) my wife inherited (jointly with an uncle) a small farm about sixty miles east of San Antonio, Texas. Because of family bickering (due to the belief that there was oil beneath the farmland) a lawsuit was filed contesting the will. In order to be on top of the problem we decided to relocate from California to Texas. We were under the impression that things could be settled easily, and we would soon be able to return to our California lifestyle. In the course of events additional adjoining parcels of land were also added to the inheritance, compounding the problem. We soon found that the lawsuit would demand both time and money, so we both took jobs and settled down to await the outcome.

I had several short-lived jobs, but my wife remained employed as a waitress at a recently built hotel. We were forced by our financial condition to take a one-room apartment about five blocks from The Alamo. We were encouraged by my wife's father to go to church (he was a Southern Baptist missionary on the island of Shodashima in the sea of Japan). We responded to his advice, and started to attend the Little Church of La Vita, the first church ever built in San Antonio.

One Sunday morning the minister stopped us as we left the church and asked if we might come to his soup kitchen (Loaves and Fishes) to have a talk. When this meeting took place he recommended that we go to the church (around the corner) and pray that we would do whatever God wanted us to do. This we did at his request.

A few days later one of my wife's aunts invited my wife, my daughter and myself to dinner. This was an invitation we gratefully accepted. Upon arrival the aunt told us to be comfortable while she made a fast trip to the market.

Darafina and the Ouija Board

As our daughter Deanna watched television, my wife and I sat on the couch surrounded by sewing machines. These machines were used by the aunt to teach sewing classes. It was then my wife spotted a Ouija board propped against one of the machines. With a laugh she brought it to the couch and placed it between us. Immediately upon putting our fingers on the planchette it began to move. It spelled out, "Buy your own board. Pay for it with silver." I, of course, thought this message was produced for some reason by my wife; she in turn believed *I* was its author. The message was repeated once more, and then the board seemed to go mute.

After dinner we asked the aunt if she thought there was any validity to the messages of a Ouija board. She was a believer, and she proceeded to use it, with my wife asking questions. After hearing how we would all have a rich and wonderful future, I concluded that the messages of the Ouija board were nothing more than a means for the subconscious to spell out a person's hopes and dreams. This belief I kept to myself.

It was necessary that I walk each day several blocks to a small market to purchase food with my wife's tip money. It usually took every cent she made in one day to feed the three of us for that day. Several days after the Ouija board incident she arrived home with about $3 more than usual. She asked me if I thought this was an indication from God that we should buy a Ouija board? I said no, and recommended instead an air-conditioned movie as a relief from the hot and humid Texas summer weather of 1963.

The very next day on my return from the market, as I stepped off a curb I spied three new $1 bills rolled in a ball lying in the gutter. Upon returning home I announced my windfall. My wife Jo Nell looked at me long and hard and then said, "I think this means we should buy a Ouija board."

We decided we would pray about the matter and did. It was then Jo Nell reached in her apron pocket and pulled out a dime that had been lodged in the pocket's corner. We now had $3.10 to our name. I took the dime and called the department store (Joskie's of Texas) to find that they had Ouija boards in their toy department for $2.98 (there was no sales tax in Texas at the time). After learning this, my daughter and I walked Jo Nell to work (she had switched to nights) and converted the $3 in bills to quarters and dimes.

After buying the Ouija board we returned to our apartment. Knowing that my 6-year-old daughter could not yet spell well or have any reason to fool her daddy, I decided to test the board with her. As soon as we put our fingers on the planchette it spelled out, "I am Darafina." It was then that a strange feeling came over me. Everything in the room that was light in color became dark and vice versa (like a photographic negative). During this phenomenon I seemed to hear my daughter's voice coming from far away, saying, "What did it say, daddy? What did it say?"

When I recovered from the shock I put the board back into its box and shoved it under the bed.

About eleven o'clock that evening my heavy thoughts were interrupted by the sound of my wife coming up the fire escape. When she entered the room she looked at me and then immediately asked, "What's wrong with you?" I told her of the test and of my experience. We then retrieved the Ouija board and placed it between us on the bed.

Until dawn of the next day we were in awe of the disembodied spirit who called herself Darafina and who accurately quoted passages from the Bible. She told us that in many previous lives we had been friends. Every free minute after that night we sat as Darafina spelled out stories of our past lives that took place on a distant planet. The heat of the non-air-conditioned room caused us to drip perspiration on the board. Darafina recommended that we sprinkle talcum powder on the board so that the planchette would glide easier. On one very hot day the plastic planchette began to soften in the heat to the point that impressions of our fingertips became part of its surface. (I must pause to say that neither one of us were versed in scripture, so we were convinced that neither one of us was secretly playing games.) Darafina frightened us. We accused her of being sent by the devil, for we knew even the devil can quote scripture.

Darafina insisted on calling my wife Arranella, my daughter Falshakina, and me Reyatis. She told us that these were the names she knew us by in previous lives.

Darafina prophesied that Jo Nell would be put in charge of the hotel dining room, and that due to circumstances beyond the control of the adversarial relatives the lawsuit would be dropped. Both of these things happened within days of Darafina saying them. In addition, Darafina would give us the subject of the upcoming Sunday sermon at the Little Church, even though the pastor prided himself on not preparing a sermon in advance, speaking only as the spirit moved him at the time.

Jo Nell began to write down each and every question asked and every answer or story that Darafina told us.

When Darafina was asked what she looked like, she said she had long red hair and was wearing a green gown. When she was asked where she was, she first said she was riding around on the planchette. Then she said she was sitting on a rock on the far side of the River Styx waiting to return to living human form.

After several months of hypnotically watching the planchette move from letter to letter, I began to realize that I knew what was going to be said *before* the answer spelled out. This I confessed to my wife.

I then began to think that all the stories and information that had come to us on the board previously was somehow a figment of my imagination. But how could I prophesy things so accurately? My wife said: "If this is coming out of you, let's not stop. You have become more interesting than you have ever been."

We soon realized that I could not mentally answer a question put to Darafina unless we first worked with the Ouija board for about 10 minutes. Thereafter the board was not necessary. The mental response I got from questions asked of Darafina would rise like a thought expressed in my own mental voice. I also found that I could allow the "thought message" to directly trigger my physical vocal cords. I did not care for this, because many of Darafina's feminine mannerisms accompanied her transmissions, and caused me to feel and act strange in public.

At Darafina's direction, we asked for and received a loan ($3000) on the farm from the lawyer who handled our case. This was in September 1963.

We then bought a used car, loaded up our belongings and headed west. It was our desire to return to California, but Darafina insisted that we first visit my parents, sister and brother-in-law in Idaho Falls, Idaho. In the course of our travels two things occurred. First, I noticed that just before and after we passed under high-voltage power lines I could not hear or feel Darafina. At Darafina's insistence, Jo Nell bought a pair of soft, orange leather sandals. (The purchase of these sandals will be mentioned again later.)

On to Idaho Falls

En route we came to a stop in Las Vegas, Nevada. Here I began to play blackjack with Darafina's assistance. Betting only a dollar or two a hand, after a full night of playing my winnings eventually approached about $800. My thoughts of that evening were to leave Las Vegas and head directly to California. Thinking this way proved to be a big mistake. By dawn, after I had downed numerous brandy eggnogs, a woman walked up to the table and asked if she could bet $10 on my hand. I said yes. I then began to lose and lose and lose. I could no longer mentally hear Darafina and get her advice. Soon I was betting large amounts of our own money and still losing. I got hold of my senses just in time. After counting the money that was left, I realized that I still had enough to pay the hotel bill and get either to Los Angeles or Idaho Falls.

I returned to the hotel room to find my sleeping wife and daughter. After telling them of my foolishness, we took out the Ouija board and asked Darafina what to do. Her answer was, "I told you that you must first go to Idaho." We left Las Vegas just before dark and headed north toward Salt Lake City. As our daughter Deanna slept in the back seat, my wife sat beside me and wept. I never felt so bad in all my life.

We had just passed through the town of Mesquite, Nevada, when suddenly I heard an audible male voice say, "This is copy 67. This is the mother. This is the Regulas. This is the old Queen of the Stars, but the new stars look also to her peaceful way. Where is my darling?"

I quickly turned to see if someone had somehow gotten into the back seat. I also checked to see if the radio was on, but it wasn't. I asked Jo Nell if she'd heard the voice, but she said that she had not.

A very angry-feeling Darafina arose in my mind, stating with strong emotion, "Don't talk to them! That's none of your business. You have intercepted a telepathic conversation between people who are not from the earth. If you talk to them you will be sorry." In a matter of minutes an audible voice repeated its previous message only to be answered by another male voice, which said, "This is the brother of the Black Dragon. I am an eagle. Where is my mother?"

Then the original male voice once again spoke telepathically: "Is that you, Reyatis? Are Arranella and Falashakina with you? I am Rosirus. I am black, I am silver. This is zero of the Regulas. If you wish to contact us in the future, think of how a piece of orange leather would look, feel, smell and taste." After telling Jo Nell of these instructions she instantly recalled the orange leather sandals that Darafina had encouraged her to buy. The fact that the telepathic spaceman called us by the same names that Darafina called us was also quite bewildering. Somehow I could sense a plot thickening.

We stopped by the side of the road. The clear night sky was filled with stars, and we could see nothing moving among them. Through the remainder of the night there was not a word from either the space people or Darafina.

Simple Songs Please Will You Sing

Upon reaching Idaho Falls, we were received wonderfully. It had been several years since we had visited with my parents and my younger sister's family.

From the beginning of our visit, Jo Nell and I looked daily for excuses to leave the house and drive to some remote spot where we could park and use the Ouija board. Most of Darafina's messages were warnings about how miserable we would be if we contacted the extraterrestrials. When asked why the extraterrestrials called us by the same names she did, and why they told me to use the orange-leather mental picture to reestablish contact with them, she said: "You *might* understand these things at some time in the future, but not yet."

It came to pass that my brother-in-law Bill asked Jo Nell and me to accompany him to sell a car in the town of Blackfoot (south of Idaho Falls). The sale did not come off, and as we drove home there was very little conversation. I looked over toward Bill, whose face was bathed in the soft lights of the dashboard. As I did he began to relate the subject of a dream he had been having every night for weeks prior to our arrival. He said he stopped having the dream only after we showed up. Bill worked for the Westinghouse Nuclear Facility located in the desert about 80 miles west of Idaho Falls. In his dream he is returning from work on the shuttle bus, when he is seized by the impulse to get up from his seat and request the driver to stop the bus. He leaves the bus and walks across the desert dunes. There he sees an alien spaceship waiting for him. At this point in the dream he wakes up.

Jo Nell and I (after a few coded words between us) decided to tell Bill about our using the Ouija board, but not about Darafina or what she had been saying. We asked him if there would be any objection to our bringing the Ouija board into the house. He said there would be no problem whatsoever.

That night we placed the board on the kitchen table between my sister Pat and her husband Bill. As my mother, Jo Nell and I looked on, the planchette began to move, spelling out, "I am Darafina."

Jo Nell quickly turned to her notebook where among its pages was recorded Darafina's name hundreds of times. A strange look came over their faces as the stark reality of it all began to set in.

Within the next few days there was not a Ouija board to be found for sale within hundreds of miles of Idaho Falls. The house was now filled with young married couples sitting everywhere with Ouija boards between them. The nature of the messages they were receiving were in some cases insulting and accusatory of each other. I felt Darafina doing mental cartwheels within my head. She said, "It's now time to move to your own place."

Within days I acquired a job delivering auto parts for a Dodge dealership. We moved into an apartment for rent by the week that was directly across the street from my job.

One evening just after coming home from work and while waiting for dinner to be prepared, I was shocked to hear the telepathic voice of Rosirus requesting to talk to my wife. He refused to talk to me without her being present. This led to his request to give me a number of mental tests. We agreed, and the tests began and continued night after night. These tests were in the form of unique prose, such as:

"Simple songs please will you sing. Rest in hills never known for peace. 666. Blasting orange. Call left. Kile matrons breed noises and mistakes. There are now bellows from militant oxen. Yes, black prince, I love your birth. Protecting lions and jackals with spots sleep beneath your cradle. Cry settler god passes and trumpets break. Why blow Jericho when Babylon's walls are now weaker? Their's will be a trough of waste that runs into time infinite. There they will find themselves bound by chains of gold-plated lead."

There were hundreds of such tests, and we were asked to comment as much as possible about each line.

I soon realized that I was unable to remember any of the communications, and had to rely on Jo Nell to repeat (from her notes) what had been said. This was frustrating, because the communications and Jo Nell's recaps took hours.

During communication I could not wear a ring or watch, for after a period of time they produced a discomforting heat. If an electric motor started up during the course of communication my spinal nerves would jump.

I eventually came to hate even the thought of communication with the extraterrestrials. Even though this was my feeling at the time, I can presently say that I would not have missed that experience for anything in the world.

Resorting once again to the Ouija board and Darafina, we were met by the statement, "I am Darafina. I am leaving. Goodbye." The Ouija board never spelled out a message for us again.

Spacecraft Demonstrations

One late afternoon in November 1963, I received a communication that instructed us to drive to the base of the foothills east of town. I gathered up my parents and other relatives and departed for the area. Upon arrival I was telepathically instructed to look up. There in the twilight was a silver-colored disk zig-zagging slowly across the sky. My father peered through a pair of binoculars, then passed them on for others to use. The spacecraft suddenly sped away in a straight line to the east. Further communication instructed us to relocate to a point on the bluffs east of the Snake River. Bill instinctively knew the way.

We parked on a road leading to a closed ski lodge and lift. We ignored the cold as we watched for more than an hour as an alien spacecraft stopped, zig-zagged, climbed, disappeared and reappeared. Then came the communication: "We will now cease to demonstrate the abilities of this vehicle." The craft then disappeared from sight.

An Ancient Statue

Not working the next day, some of us drove to the western side of the Snake River bluffs (across the river from the sighting location). I felt drawn to the place. As we walked along the high cliffs, my mother bent over and picked up a small rock that resembled the foot (with toes) of a small statue. Everyone pitched in to dig and soon additional pieces of the statue came to light.

Before leaving the area our attention was drawn to the cliff on the far side of the river. There in the face of the cliff was what appeared to be a carving of a stick figure of a man. We made note of this for future exploration.

After returning home we reassembled the statue, finding it to be about 2-1/2 feet tall. In its hands was a bowl that we were able to fill with small stones that were shaped like kernels of corn. We affectionately referred to the statue as "Sam."

The local newspaper got wind of our find and published Sam's picture along with our account of his discovery. This brought a visit from a number of anthropologists from the state university. After we took them to the discovery site, they notified us that if we continued to dig in the area we would be in violation of a number of federal laws. Shortly after taking Sam with them, they proceeded to surround the area with a chain link fence and "no trespassing" signs.

The Mountain Doorway

As soon as time permitted we took up exploration of the cliffs on the eastern side of the Snake River, concentrating on the area of the stick figure. It was at this time that we made a very important discovery.

It was quite apparent that one section of the grey basalt cliff had been filled in by red rocks. The filled-in area resembled what appeared to have once been an opening or doorway into the mountain. Our compass spun in its casing, endlessly searching for magnetic north. Driving down the frontage road that exists between the "doors" and the river, we found the figure of a Chinese-type dragon painted on the rock face of the cliff. We took black-and-white pictures of both sites and studied them carefully. Close analysis revealed the "doors" were framed by the carved figures of a man and woman. No less than seven carved faces were also found situated above the doors. Some of the carved figures were adorned with plumed helmets (similar to headgear worn by the ancient Romans and Greeks).

Chatter Box

Returning to the fall of 1963: I was tormented by the persistence of the extraterrestrials in communicating to me in such a way that I could not recall what had been said during the session. One night I came out of the communication state to learn that we had been in contact not only with the extraterrestrials, but also with a group of earth telepaths who worked for the United States government. This group of telepaths were code-named Chatter Box. I later learned that this group was based on the Caribbean Island of Grand Turk. I was surprised to also learn during the session that one of the Chatter Box group had been telepathically transmitting the words of the then President of the United States, John F. Kennedy. This telepathic conversation ended with an agreement between the President and the extraterrestrials to physically cooperate in the future, followed by a period during which the President would decide how to inform the American people of the existence and purposes of the extraterrestrials. Two days after this telepathic agreement was made, John Kennedy was assassinated in Dallas, Texas.

Several days after the death of President Kennedy and the assassination of Lee Harvey Oswald the extraterrestrials instructed us to leave Idaho Falls and go to Los Angeles.

12
Yesteryear, A Million Times Yesteryear

June 1992

In early November 1963, when I was living in Idaho Falls, my telepathic contact with the extraterrestrials was being painstakingly developed. It was at this time that they chose to give my wife and me a physical sighting of one of their spacecraft to prove that they were more than a voice in my head or some figment of my imagination.

After a night of observing an extraterrestrial spacecraft perform maneuvers that defied the presently accepted laws of aerodynamics, a group of us returned the following day to the Snake River cliffs directly across the river from the sighting area. It was on this day that two very exciting things occurred: Pieces of a two-foot-tall statue were found by my mother, and after a binocular scan of the opposing cliffs at the river I noticed that there was a rectangular patch of red rock that looked unnatural in the gray-colored rock that surrounded it.

A few days later we went to the area of the red patch to inspect it up close. At once we recognized that the rectangular red patch of stone filled in what was *once a doorway into the face of the cliff*. Furthermore, we found that this "doorway" was flanked by eroded columns similar to those used in other types of ancient architecture. Right and left of the columns were, respectively, the carved head of a woman and that of a helmeted man atop the head of a primitive-looking humanoid. Above the doorway was a field of seven carved faces, six facing right and one facing left.

We also noticed that at some time in history someone had attempted to tunnel into the doors at the upper left corner. Only about five feet of tunnel remained at its entrance. It is possible that the tunnel was longer at one time, but later collapsed. This tunnel provided us with two pieces of information: (1) The red rock seal was only about a foot thick. (2) The material behind the red rock was decomposed granite, which obviously was deposited by floodwaters into any hollow area(s) that once existed beyond the red rock seal. (A plan is in mind to use water from the nearby Snake River pumped at high pressure to wash away the decomposed granite and thus restore to their original size and shape any chambers that are found within.)

As we stood in front of the doors one of the men in our party called our attention to his compass. We all watched in amazement as the needle spun rapidly in circles. Later extraterrestrial telepathic contact informed us that *behind the doors exists a small space vehicle that is still operable.*

The Dragon Painting

(See Figs. 1 & 2)

Down the cliff to the left of the doors we found a 25-foot-tall painting of a dragon (or possibly a seahorse). Farther away, about two hundred yards left of the doors, we found carvings on the cliff wall of a man sitting on a throne with others kneeling before him. The seated figure seemed to be wearing a pillbox hat and robes reminiscent of those worn in ancient Sumeria.

The following pictures were taken in the summer of 1972, nine years after our first visit. (I regret that the pictures of the seated man have become lost over the years.)

The Doors

(See Figs. 3 & 4)

This photograph of the doors was taken from about 150 yards. It gives a full view of the doors and contains all of the following features. **1, 2** and **3:** The three doors of red stone. The center door is about 25 feet wide and 25 feet high and is flanked by columns **4** and **5**. This center door appears to be the key point of entry, as it is flanked by carved heads;

seven heads also appear directly above it. Next, **6** is the image of a helmeted head above a primitive humanoid head, both facing right; **7**, a woman's head, highly eroded, facing left; and **8**, seven heads above the central door, facing right.

Faces
(See Figs. 5 & 6)

In the left third of this picture can be found the images of a **helmeted man** above a primitive-looking (animal-like) head. Slightly to the left of the mouth of the primitive head stands my daughter Deanna whose 5' 2" height permitted me to estimate the head to be about 5' high and 3-1/2' wide. By the same means I estimated the helmeted head above to be about the same size. Both heads face what was once a vertically straight **architectural column**. This column presently rises unevenly, due to earth shifts over time. To the right of the column, wearing white and standing within the frame of the central door, is Cindia Hannah. In the top left corner of the door, directly over Cindia, can be seen the dark **tunnel entrance**.

Woman and Column
(See Figs. 7 & 8)

In this picture Cindia sits with her back to the architectural column to the right of the center door. Directly above her outstretched arm is the chin and nose of what was obviously once the carved face of a woman whose forehead and cranium are still distinguishable.

Seven Faces and Door
(See Figs. 9 & 10)

This picture shows the field of seven sculpted faces, all apparently masculine. Although there are seven faces, only four are clear enough to be referenced in the photograph.

As the years have gone by I have often thought of the Idaho doors, and on one occasion telepathically asked a personal extraterrestrial friend why I was told of this ancient site and its long-buried spacecraft. His first reply, accompanied by laughter was: "That craft is your way home." His second reply was more serious: "This site might someday help to prove that you are in contact with us and that all the information we have imparted to you should be taken very seriously by those with whom you have shared the information. Furthermore, there may regretfully come a time that the exact location of this site might be traded for your physical freedom or the physical freedom of others of the Light."

When I asked how old the site was, he replied: "Older than the Great Pyramid of Egypt and older than the 500,000-year-old face and buildings that are found at Cydonia on the planet Mars. One can truly say that the doors are of yesteryear, a million times yesteryear."

It is in my mind to some day revisit the Idaho doors and attempt to recover the buried spacecraft and any other pre-Frequency Barrier artifacts that might be recoverable. That expedition will have to be perfectly planned and executed so as to not invite the negative attention of several of our distrustful government agencies – that is, those in the government who believe that our knowledge of our ancient past would jeopardize their present control and their plans for stricter control over us in the future.

Fig. 1.

Fig. 2. Artists rendering of the area in Fig 1

Fig. 1. The image of the dragon can be seen between blocks C through H vertically and 4 through 8 horizontally. Based on the six-foot figure standing at the base of the dragon painting, it is estimated that the image is about 25 feet high. The painting was as vivid in 1972 as it was in 1963. (I would really like to know the formula of this paint.)

The curved neck of the animal in the painting suggests that it might be a seahorse. The outline of the lower end of the animal, after turning upward, continues for over 150 feet up the side of the hill. Here and there the painting was broken up by cracks in the stone surface due to earth movement over the years.

I believe the image is of a dragon because the dragon symbolizes the revolving high-temperature plasma component of the propulsion system of an extraterrestrial spacecraft. This symbol might therefore be related to the fact that such a spacecraft is parked behind the doors. (See my book Dragons and Chariots.*)*

Fig. 3. There are actually three doors, which extend from about 3–13, I-K. From the left, ***door 1*** *extends from 2-6. Thereafter* ***carved heads*** *appear in block 7 and part of block 6, J-K*

Following the carved heads to the right is the remains of what was obviously once an ***architectural column*** *between blocks 7-8, I-J. (Closeups of these heads and the column are found in other pictures.)*

To the right is ***door 2*** *(8–10)*

Above door 2 is a field of ***seven faces,*** *six facing right and one facing left (2–12, D-H).* ***The entrance and remains of the tunnel*** *are found in the upper left corner of door 2 (Block 8I).*

Right of the central door is another ***column*** *(Blocks 10-11, I-K). Following the column to the left is a highly eroded* ***head of a woman*** *(later shown as a closeup).*

To its left is ***door 3*** *(12-13, I-K.)*

Fig. 3.

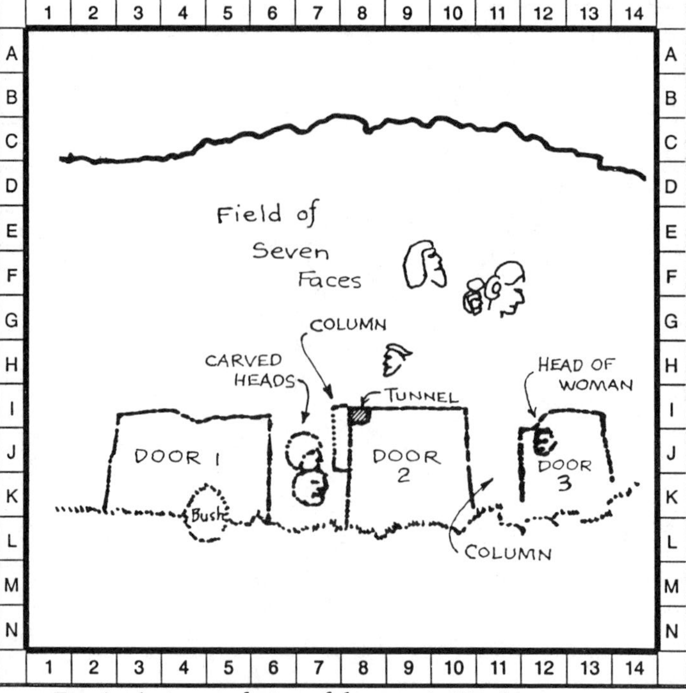

Fig. 4. Artists rendering of the area in Fig. 3.

Fig. 5.

Fig. 5. *The image of a* ***helmeted man*** *appears at 2-5, D-F. Deanna Bateman stands below the heads of the helmeted man and humanoid (3-5, G-I).*

The left column: *7-8 A-F. Cindia Hannah, wearing white, stands in the doorway just right of the left column and directly under the tunnel entrance.*

The tunnel opening: *9-10, A-B.*

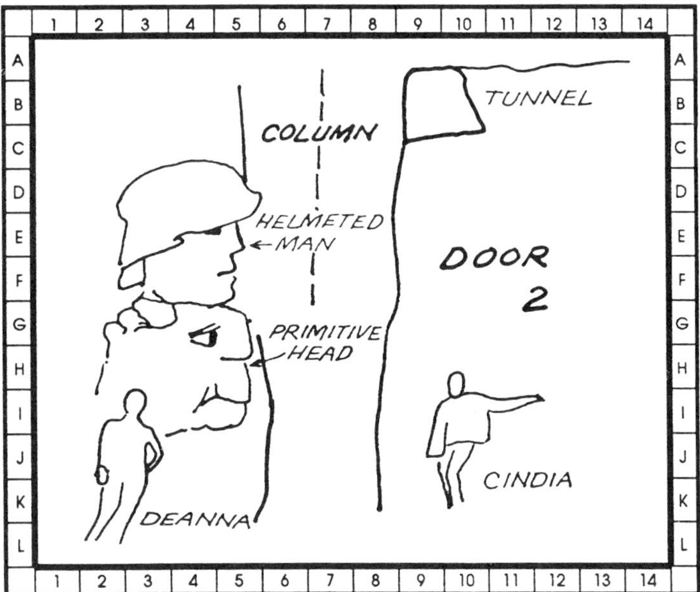

Fig. 6. Artist's rendering of the area in Fig. 5.

The right column is found at 8-9, D-H. The eroded face of a woman looking to the left extends from 10-11, E-G.

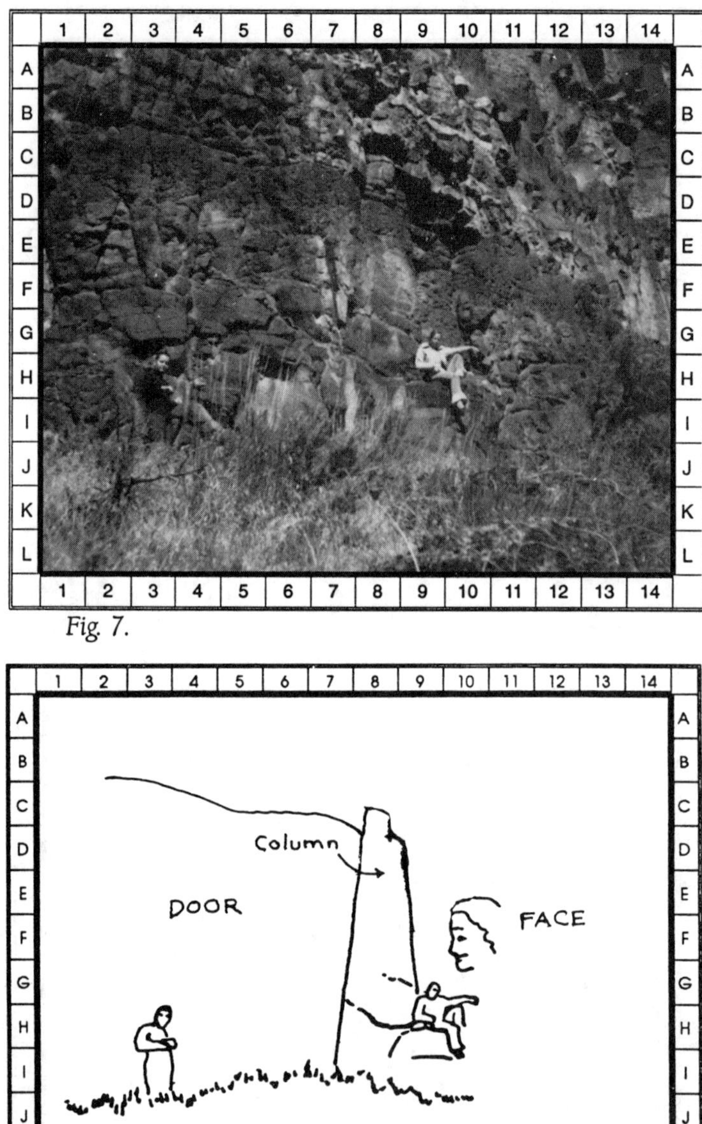

Fig. 7.

Fig. 8. Artist's rendering of the area in Fig. 7.

Fig. 9.

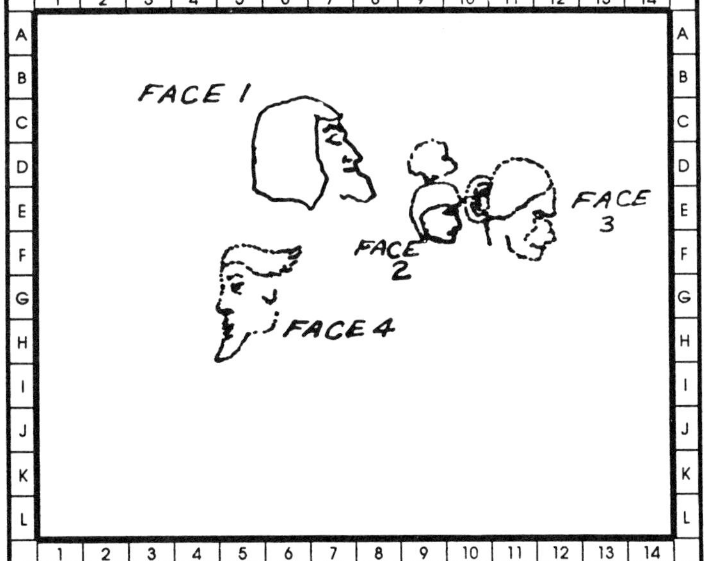

Fig. 10. Artist's rendering of the area in Fig. 9.

*Here is a field of **seven sculpted faces** over the central door (four clearer than the others) 5-15, C-H.*

***Face 1:** a long-haired, bearded man looking slightly upward (6-8, C-E).*

***Face 2:** a man wearing a plumed helmet with side straps, ancient Greek type (9-10, E-F)*

***Face 3:** a man, facing right, who wears a chignon-type hair roll at the back of his head (11-12, D-F).*

Face 4: *a bearded person facing left (5-6, F-H).*

If the pointed protrusion above the figure was once part of the sculpture, then it is possible this figure is wearing a pointed hat similar to that worn by the Catholic Pope.

Fig. 11. This photograph depicts my wife, Jo Nell, standing with the doors in the background. This picture also shows a fiery ball that passed over Jo Nell's right shoulder as the picture was snapped. Notice the glowing trail it left behind. This indicates that the object was moving quite rapidly in relationship to the camera's shutter speed. Within the glowing ball was a small monitor disc (about 8 inches in diameter). These monitor discs are sometimes called eavesdroppers and are used to record and transmit visual, audio and other forms of information to an extraterrestrial scout craft located nearby. It is evident that the extraterrestrials were watching and listening in on our conversations as we photographed this ancient site.

13

Mental Investigations Of New Dimensions

July 1992

During our stay in Idaho Falls my extraterrestrial communications left me drained of energy and emotionally disturbed. I hated to telepathically communicate to the extraterrestrials, but was urged on by my wife and the extraterrestrials' promise that this period of discomfort would not last too much longer.

Choosing to Stay or Leave Earth

I felt that I was in a state of constant physical and emotional torment. Then one day the extraterrestrials stated: "If you can't take it anymore, maybe we should physically pick up you and your family from the earth."

I took them up on their offer and the next day drove in mid-afternoon to a designated pick-up spot about 20 miles from town. The sky that day was grey and overcast. We had been directed to drive to the end of a dirt road and park. Before us was a plowed field bordered on the far side by a row of trees. We were very nervous as we listened telepathically to the extraterrestrials remind us why we were on the Earth in the first place, and that we were throwing away an important spiritual opportunity by leaving.

Then a circular spacecraft (about 50 feet in diameter) appeared above the nearby trees, as if by materialization, bending them as it hovered. The craft was black without markings. The spacecraft then moved toward us and hovered over the middle of the field. Telepathically we were told to leave the car and walk to the craft, or if we wished to change our minds and stay on the Earth, this was our last chance to say so. After being racked by every kind of emotion including fear, we hastily decided to remain on the Earth. Upon hearing our decision the spacecraft slowly gained altitude, then suddenly disappeared. This event was followed by an extraterrestrial instruction to leave Idaho Falls and go to Los Angeles

Relocations

Upon arriving in Los Angeles in the winter of 1963 both my wife and I found jobs. After a several-month stay in Los Angeles the extraterrestrials told us to relocate to Palm Springs, California. This we did as soon as possible.

In Palm Springs we both found new jobs in two different resort hotels. My wife JoNell worked at the Palm Springs Spa and I at the Riviera. It was during the Palm Springs period that the extraterrestrials finally began to answer my many questions: (1) Do you know if there is a God? (2) Do you know if there is life after death? (3) How is telepathy possible? (4) Why do I sometimes get a numbing, blank feeling in my brain during telepathic communication? (5) Why don't I remember what was said during a telepathic session? (6) Why are you communicating to me, and are you also communicating in the same way with other people on the Earth?

The Universal Life Field

The extraterrestrials told us that they knew beyond doubt that there was a Supreme God who was responsible for everything that exists. They told us of the existence of the "Omnipresent, All-Permeating Universal Life Field" (ULF) and its multilevels of perception (dimensions). They explained to us how the Supreme Creator, the Els and all other beings (alive, disembodied, or reperfected) functioned in the ULF.

They explained that telepathy was possible because all life is linked together on various levels of the ULF. With knowhow, two or more people (alive or disembodied) can align themselves perfectly on the same level of perception of the ULF and therefore telepathically communicate. They explained that it took them millions of years to learn how to accomplish this kind of mental synchronization and put it into common use.

The Patrax

The extraterrestrials told us that reembodiment as a human being occurs again and again, and after the very first life, an individual psyche follows a "destiny pattern." These patterns help a person to subconsciously bring forth training and talents that were strongly developed in previous lifetimes. They also informed us that in my case, I had developed an exceptional telepathic ability over many previous lifetimes, and for that reason embodied within the frequency barrier of the Earth in order to play a part in a divinely inspired plan called "the Patrax." They went on to explain that there many Patrax people, but not all develop telepathy. Many possess other abilities that will be eventually awakened within them and later employed for the good of the Patrax. The extraterrestrials went on to say that many Patrax sleepers will awaken when they learn of the ULF, Els, frequency barrier, "charge force" and the "other side of the wheel," and it was my job to see that they heard of these things.

During the time my family and I spent in Palm Springs a restriction was removed from the telepathic procedure. I was now able to remember everything that was said during a telepathic session. This revealed that over the period of time the restriction was in place I had developed a very good memory. From that time to this day I have not forgotten one single detail pertaining to any subject we had telepathically discussed with the extraterrestrials.

How Telepathy Works

The extraterrestrials asked me not to read any books on UFOs, ESP or metaphysics. The reason they gave for making this request was to prevent me from acquiring any "false references." A telepath with too many false references about a particular subject is not worth the effort, or *charge force* (psychic energy), it would take to pursue the subject matter telepathically.

The extraterrestrials explained that the occasional numbing, blank feeling I sometime felt in my head during a telepathic session was due to the fact that I had no conscious reference to what was being transmitted; thus the brain was responding in a "dumbfounded" manner. This phenomenon was additionally explained in the following way: Think of a white elephant. When a person mentally visualizes a white elephant, they first search their mental inventory for the color white and the image they know to be that of an elephant. Assembling these two references collectively in the mind's eye brings forth the image of a white elephant. When a person is asked to think of something such as an "Abarb" and finds no mental references, the mind remains blank, or dumbfounded. If the person was told that an Abarb was a mythological animal that looked like a little green dog with feet like a duck, these references will be recalled every time the name "Abarb" is mentioned or thought of.

When I asked how their spacecraft operated, they advised me to acquire as many references as possible on the subject of high-temperature plasma containment (plasma being the fourth state of matter). This I did. Each night for nearly a year thereafter I fell asleep telepathically communicating on the subject of extraterrestrial propulsion systems. The more I learned about plasma containment, the better my understanding of saucer propulsion became. (For information pertaining to spacecraft propulsion systems, see my book *Dragons and Chariots*.)

The term for the type of telepathy being explained is called "copy and cancel telepathy." A second, more efficient and less charge-costing form of telepathy called "zero-zero telepathy" will be described in a later article.

The Universal Psychic Language

Telepathic communications are accomplished by synchronizing the minds of the participants at the same place in the *micro* level of perception (dimension of the ULF). Spoken language, or the language that a telepath thinks in, makes no difference, as thoughts (in any language) translate automatically into the universal psychic language inherent in every person who exists. For example, if a telepath thinking in Spanish transmits the thought of a table (called *mesa* in Spanish), the thought of the *mesa* is automatically translated into the universal psychic language. When the thought reaches a person who thinks in English, the transmission in the psychic language is retranslated to the English word *table*.

One of the proofs that a universal language exists within us all comes from a study conducted by the United Nations. In this study it was found that the first word an infant utters is "Mama" no matter what its race or where the child was born. It was also shown in this study that infants (also uncoached) will, upon seeing their father, respond with the word "Dada." These are, of course, only two examples. The extraterrestrials tell us that an infant born on any planet in the universe will, without being taught, call their parents Mama and Dada.

The extraterrestrials have been able to identify the mental images of the universal psychic language with corresponding spoken words (also the written word); thus they really *are* saying what they think. The psychic language in the form of the spoken word is called Soltec Mal. Human thought waves (synonymous with the psychic language) are universal; that is, even though spoken languages are not compatible, the mental waves (on the psychic level) of every human are identical. Using an instrument that compares the mental symbolism of two individuals (not speaking the same language) and finding that their mental symbols match is an indication that the two individuals have a precise understanding. Because this type of brain-wave comparison is possible, the extraterrestrials use it to prepare contracts and agreements. Extraterrestrial telepaths have on occasion asked to be forgiven for not making some point perfectly clear due to the fact that their ability to speak (think) in Soltec was not the best.

Copy and Cancel Telepathy

Returning to the subject of *copy and cancel telepathy,* the following mental phenomena also pertain: (1) Cancellation to the nearest mental reference. In this case a person might not have the mental reference for an orange and therefore might falsely cancel the telepathic symbol as an apple, which is also a fruit. A second example: Let's say the telepathic transmitter wishes to impart information about a bottle of amber-colored glue. The receiver, not having the references for glue, might falsely cancel the symbolic references (and subreferences) as molasses, which is also amber in color and sticky. After drawing flies to something the receiver tried to stick together, the receiver might come to the conclusion that someone was pulling his or her leg.

The state of technology is an important thing to consider when telepathy is concerned. Imagine a primitive receiver trying to comprehend electricity. Not having the mental reference for electricity but understanding that it can produce light, might relate the symbolic transmission to a torch or (if the receiver were a little more advanced technically) a candle. I have often wished I had a head full of medical references so that I might bring through (telepathically) cures for many of the diseases that now plague the people of this world. (A booklet describing telepathy and other so-called psi phenomena in detail is about to be written.)

My First Book

After a considerable period of telepathic communication with the extraterrestrials (while living in Palm Springs) the extraterrestrials suggested that we write a book about what we had learned from them up to that time. My wife and I collectively wrote the book and called it *Giant Step*.

During the writing of *Giant Step* we heard of George Van Tassel, who operated the Giant Rock airport near Yucca Valley, California. We also learned that he claimed to have had physical contact with extraterrestrials. We were surprised to find that our extraterrestrial telepathic contacts did not object to our visiting the airport cafe where Mr. Van Tassel often spoke of his UFO experiences. We were permitted to go to Giant Rock on the condition that we would listen but not relate that we were also in contact with extraterrestrials.

Upon our arrival we found a large Marine helicopter parked beside the airstrip in front of the cafe. Inside Mr. Van Tassel was telling the chopper's crew of six about his UFO sightings and contacts. The looks on the crewmen's faces ranged from total disbelief to amusement. It was our hope that we did not have to present our story publicly, because we did not feel we could handle the smirks and ridicule. We listened as we ate our lunch, and left while Mr. Van Tassel's lecture was still under way.

While driving home we discussed what we had heard and witnessed. Mr. Van Tassel claimed that he had physically met extraterrestrials—face to face—and continued to telepathically communicate with them on a daily basis. We were quite confused, as we had been told by the extraterrestrials that a physical contact was not possible due to the existence of the frequency barrier.

Claims of ET Contact

We learned that telling people about personal extraterrestrial contact was no easy matter, and to do so took a lot of guts. Over the years I have encountered many people who had some degree of true telepathic contact with the extraterrestrials and others who *thought* they did. I also encountered some who made these claims and were nothing more than con artists and snake-oil salesmen.

Over the last thirty years it has been my goal to gather as much physical evidence as possible to support my claim of telepathic contact with the extraterrestrials. With their assistance I feel I have been able to compile a considerable amount of supportive evidence such as (1) predictions of earthquakes and their corresponding UFO-sighting locations on Los Angeles television (in 1965 – Attorney Melvin Belli was the host); (2) revelation of the extraterrestrial means of spacecraft propulsion (acclaimed by Willard Libby, Nobel Prize winner in physics, the A.E.C. and the Soviet Academy of Science); (3) newspaper documentation of earthquakes and UFO sightings (frequency barrier related – see earlier article); (4) the finding of Flight 19 (see earlier article); (5) explanations of livestock mutilations (see earlier Dulce base article); (6) the Idaho "doors" (see earlier article); and (7) the 17-year pyramid-research project that resulted in the writing of the 3-volume series *The Rods of Amon Ra*. The mathematical deductions found in *The Rods of Amon Ra* were used by a French/Egyptian archeological team to locate a hidden chamber in the Great Pyramid of Giza, and on the basis of this find I was invited by the Egyptian Antiquities Organization to speak at a symposium in Cairo in December 1987.

A Period of Nightmares, Then Zero-Zero Contact

During the Palm Springs period I went through terrifying nightly experiences of falling into a black abyss, my body totally paralyzed. Only an extreme effort to move a body part stopped the frightening falling effect. Many persons have related that they have had this happen to them. These nightly occurrences stopped after several months when on one afternoon I took a nap. When it began again, I allowed the falling effect to continue without making an attempt to stop it. The result was a loud crackling sound at the base of my skull.

Thereafter the extraterrestrials began to develop a "zero-zero" telepathic relationship with me. This permits instant telepathic contact without the use of large amounts of psychic energy (charge force). Upon the activation of the telepathic channel there is a mental buzz. When one tries to identify this buzz as a feeling, it is more like a sound. When one tries to identify this buzz as a sound, its character changes to a feeling. (Zero-zero telepathy, along with an explanation of the terms "ava-trending" and "dea-trending," will be covered in my next article.)

My wife JoNell and I wrote the book *Giant Step* in longhand and sought someone to type it. The typing task was taken on by Maxine Kester, who was the executive secretary to the manager of the Palm Springs Spa Hotel where my wife was employed as a waitress. As Maxine typed the material, she was moved by it and suggested that we attend a New Age-type gathering that was held once a week at the home of Paul and Mildred Summit.

New Sightings and Messages

Paul and Mildred asked us to dinner one evening along with an elderly lady named Violet Watson. At dusk we gathered on their rooftop patio. As we talked I occupied myself by looking in different directions and observing bats alter their flight paths to line up along my line of sight. It was at this time that the extraterrestrial telepathically contacted me and gave us a message to look to the north.

There in the sky were two moving spots of light heading in our direction. After enlarging to the size of a dime, one craft took off in a streak to our left over the mountains. The other remained stationary and flashed brilliantly every time I requested that it do so. This showed without any doubt that there was contact between the craft and me. After this period of flashing, the craft started toward us and silently passed directly over our heads, disappearing over the southern horizon. The extraterrestrials informed us that they would repeat the same actions on the following night. This they did for a crowd of nearly 25 people who had crowded themselves onto the roof patio. These sightings were overwhelming for the witnesses. All signed notarized affidavits as to what they saw.

During the following year two more prearranged extraterrestrial spacecraft sightings took place on the Summit's rooftop patio. On at least one occasion Mrs. Nancy Honnicut and her husband, Col. Adolph Honnicut of the U.S. Marines, were present as a fiery disc rotated above our heads. (Nancy later became the wife of Bill Monroe, founder of The Monroe Institute of Faber, Virginia.) After more than 25 years Nancy and I had a chance to recall our mutual experiences when I was her guest at the Institute for a week in September 1990.

On a humorous note, I recall a night in which my wife and I sat poolside with two of our neighbors. One, an extremely heavy man, sat in a chair facing us and the other sat on the pool steps with his feet in the water. At this moment a large, circular extraterrestrial spacecraft silently passed over head. It was so close we could see through its lighted windows. The man on the pool steps was the first to yell out, "Did you see that?" Both my wife and I had seen it clearly, but not the heavyset gentleman named Jay. He said we were all crazy, and turned his chair around just in case whatever we saw came back. Immediately after Jay became repositioned, the same craft swooped down the side of Mount San Jacinto. Everyone saw it but him. After telling him this, he never spoke to us again.

One afternoon I was surprised to hear the telepathic voice of Darafina requesting that I call my wife into the room. She explained that she was really alive and always had been, and was sorry that she had to play the part that she did in jump-starting my telepathic abilities. She said that though she was alive at the time, her initial relationship with us was conducted while she was in a "true 90 state," a state in which she communicated to us while her psyche was out of her physical body.

At one point a friend from work who had an interest in UFOs told me that my wife and I should meet a woman whom he thought had the powers of witchcraft. We agreed to meet her, only to hear that she told my friend she would see us the following week in Los Angeles. We had no plans to go to Los Angeles, so we just forgot about the "witch."

The extraterrestrials, of course, told us to go to Los Angeles and give our book *Giant Step* to anyone free of charge if they would agree to print it.

On our first day in Los Angeles we were sitting in the front room of a man we had never met before. There was a knock on the door. There in the doorway was a petite, dark-haired woman who had recently met our host. She looked at my wife and me and said, "You are Wes and JoNell. Did you get my message that I would meet you here this week?"

14
Hooray For Hollywood?

September 1992

Upon our arrival in Los Angeles, my wife and I visited a number of publishers who were producing New Age material. Our offer to give them our book, *Giant Step*, at no charge was met with some suspicion in many cases. Some even turned down the offer to read the manuscript; others took a copy but never contacted us at a later time. One publisher we met was Michael X. Barton. We met Michael on our first day in Los Angeles, and he invited us to lunch at the Self Realization Health Food Restaurant. In the middle of lunch, a man burst upon the scene snapping pictures of my wife and me as fast as he could from every angle. The man was later identified as Bob Beck who, at the time, was a well-known UFO and New Age researcher. He had also been invited (unknown to us) to lunch by Michael. After lunch we went to Bob Beck's house on Cassil Street in Hollywood to continue our conversation. It was at this time the woman from Palm Springs (whom we had never met, and who had indirectly informed us – through a friend – that she would meet us in Los Angeles the following week) arrived at Bob Beck's door. She stayed only a few minutes and then left without explaining how she had known we would meet. Bob later told me that the woman had shown up at his door for the first time several days before. She introduced herself as a neighbor, and before the end of their first meeting, sexually seduced him. None of us ever saw the woman again. Michael agreed to publish

Giant Step but procrastinated for years, and eventually the subject was dropped.

After subleasing an apartment on Franklin Avenue in Hollywood, we began to learn what we could of existing UFO organizations and individuals claiming to have contact with extraterrestrials. It was a very interesting time. Michael Barton introduced us first to Clete Goddard and Ellery Woolsey, who directed the *Sons of Jared*, an organization apparently formed to wipe out anyone living in caverns under the Earth and any capitalist having more than $100.00 to his or her name. Ironically, a chief sponsor of this organization was a retired multimillionaire furniture manufacturer named O. B. La Voy.

We spent one afternoon listening to Ellery channel the Martian, Monka. It was a very intelligent communication, without a mention of the terrible subterraneans or the capitalists. At the end of Ellery's channeling session, he walked to the window and, pointing to something in the yard, said, "That's a Martian robin. It took about three days for it to fly here from Mars."

Eventually, we met O. B. La Voy in his fabulous home next to Griffith Park Observatory. At our meeting, Mr. La Voy inquired if we were really extraterrestrials responding to his "Light Signals." He had installed a revolving searchlight on his roof that flashed the Morse code message, "People from outerspace please contact me." From time to time during our acquaintance with O. B. La Voy, he would ask if we were actually extraterrestrially-born people who were here on Earth incognito.

O. B. La Voy introduced us to Dr. Stranges who had authored the books *Flying Saucerama* and *Stranger in the Pentagon*. The latter book was the story of how Dr. Stranges physically met with an extraterrestrial within the walls of the Pentagon. Dr. Stranges was, at the time, producing a movie called *Phenomenon 7.7*. He suggested that we take an office near his in the Empire Studios on Hollywood Boulevard. We did so, and Maxine Kester (from Palm Springs) took a vacation from her job to join us. Dr. Stranges still speaks at UFO conventions and speaks of his alien friend Val Thor, whom, he says, he met in the Pentagon. He also tells of the time he was taken on board an alien spacecraft. His account of using the toilet on the craft is just as amusing now as it was when Chief Standing Horse, of Perris Valley, California, a contactee of the 1960's, told the same story.

A skeptical Bob Beck continually requested to be in on one of my telepathic sessions with the extraterrestrials. The extraterrestrials finally agreed. Bob sat across from my desk and started his small tape recorder. As the session began, one by one, pictures on the walls began flying off their hooks and crashing to the floor, empty chairs tipped over, papers and pens that were on my desk, as well as the telephone, lifted off and fell to the floor. Bob simply spoke into the microphone of his tape recorder. "The phenomenon took place on November 8th, at 8: 20 P.M." He then walked to the door and left and would never discuss the event with me again.

I began to hold lectures on UFOs twice a week at the Anderson Research Center in Hollywood. At the same time, Michael Barton was preparing a manuscript entitled *The Incredible Search for Dr. Halsey.* Michael asked me to join him on an expedition to locate the crashed airplane of Dr. Wallace Halsey (the nephew of Admiral Bull Halsey of World War II fame). Michael, acting on a tip from a gold prospector from Mesquite, Nevada, believed the crashed plane was in the Virgin Mountains, just east of that town. I was interested in Michael's expedition because it was in the vicinity of Mesquite, Nevada, that I had had my first telepathic contact with extraterrestrials several years before.

The Dr. Halsey Story

Dr. Halsey, a UFO lecturer, had left Milford, Utah, flying a Piper Tri-Pacer airplane. With him was his one-time flight instructor, Harry, the owner of a flight school in Long Beach, California. Dr. Halsey's wife, Tanya, saw him off on his flight to Long Beach. The flight plan called for a landing at Delta, Utah, but this plan was aborted because of a herd of cows on the runway there. I can't remember where the plane landed for gas, but I do recall that the two men had coffee and then took off. While in flight, they received a bad-weather report from Cedar City, Utah, which they acknowledged. They were never seen or heard from again!

Michael had a publishing deal with Dr. Halsey's widow, Tanya. It was her hope that the plane and Dr. Halsey's remains could be found so she could collect on a $100,000 insurance policy. Dr. Halsey had carried several thousand dollars in cash, which the widow said would go to whoever found the plane.

Michael and I drove to Mesquite, then on to the Virgin Mountains. Our actual destination was a place called Wire Grass Ridge. It was there that the prospector had thought he'd heard a plane with engine trouble pass overhead during the night of Dr. Halsey's disappearance. Throughout the morning, Michael and I walked across the flat desert toward the mouth of a gorge that came out of the mountains. At about noon, we reached the gorge and began to hike up it. After several miles, we came to a dead end blocked off by a cliff several hundred feet high. To this day, I don't know what possessed us, but we decided to climb the cliff. About halfway up, we found that we could go neither up nor down —we were stranded on a ledge. Just as panic was beginning to set in, a whirling cloud of dust rose in front of us. The cloud resembled a figure dressed in a cowled robe (similar to that worn by a Franciscan Friar). The figure's outstretched arm pointed to our left, then disappeared. Responding to the "specter's" direction, Michael skirted along the ledge to the left to find that there was a narrow water channel. I joined him, and we continued up the channel.

On occasion, we encountered six- to eight-foot walls we would have to climb. With all of our water gone, we took to putting cool stones in our mouths as we continued our climb. At dusk we reached the top of the mountain. Our thirst was very great when we finally came upon a barrel cactus. We cut into the meat of the cactus and squeezed moisture out of chunks, which were wrapped in my shirt. This comfort was short-lived as the cactus juice caused our mouths to dry out, leaving us worse off than before. We climbed a small hill as night fell. We lay on the rocky hillside as two extraterrestrial spacecraft circled above us until dawn, like two angelic buzzards. During the night we were comforted by a light rainfall. At sunrise, we stood up and looked about to assess our situation.

From our hilltop viewpoint, we were just able to make out, in the distance, the white dot that was Michael's car. There were a number of water channels that appeared to bottom out at the desert floor. We chose one and started our descent. By the time we reached the desert, we were cut and bruised. Our clothes were torn and our shoes no longer had heels. It was about high noon when we started back across the desert. We soon were overtaken by exhaustion and lay down in a gully. We fought passing out by talking, both of us accepting the fact that this was the end of our lives. We even said goodbye to each other.

As I lay there, I heard a telepathic voice say "Get up, you fool, and start walking." I got to my feet, telling Michael I was going to try to make it to the car where there was a gallon of water in the back seat. I told him that if I made it, I'd come back. He acknowledged my words with a nod.

I began to walk, looking down at my shuffling feet. After what seemed an eternity, my path was blocked by a steep bank. When I lifted my eyes, I saw that I was standing directly in front of Mike's car. I managed to get up the bank, only to find that the car was locked. I broke the small wing window on the passenger side with a rock, then slid into the car. I felt behind the seat to find the water bottle, uncapped it, took a deep swallow and recapped the bottle before I passed out. I fell across the car's horn, sending a loud blast across the silent desert.

I was awakened by the sound of Michael knocking on the window. He said that the horn had given him hope—and the car's direction. We drove back to Mesquite and checked into a motel, ordered two gallons of iced lemonade and slept until the next day.

Prior to leaving on this expedition, Michael had asked me if the extraterrestrials would help us find Dr. Halsey's plane. The extraterrestrials responded with, "Ask Tanya Halsey what they were discussing when the car's fan belt broke." In Tanya's reply letter, she said, "We were talking about the Great Pyramid and the number 14." As we entered the car to leave Mesquite for Hollywood, I received this message: "Tell Michael to remember that pyramids and the number 14 will solve the Halsey Mystery". (There will be more said about this message later).

On arrival in Hollywood, we looked terrible—sunburned, with large blisters around our mouths. My wife told me, "This is the last time you're going to do something like that!" She also said that one of my students had called to ask if she could bring a recent acquaintance to my class the following evening. My wife replied that it would be all right.

It was very difficult conducting that class. During the question-and-answer part of the evening, a man (the guest of my student) kept asking questions, to the point of irritation. His last question was, "Where are all the people? In my opinion, this information should be shared by everyone." This gentleman introduced himself as Lynn Gibbs and was later instrumental in bringing about many things, such as the establishment of Mental Investigations of New Dimensions (the Mind Research Foundation and Center of Hollywood).

One afternoon as I sat at my desk, my attention was drawn to my wrap-around (bow-shaped) sunglasses. Suddenly, they began to spin clockwise on their nose bridge, while my wife and I watched with amazement. I mentally willed the glasses to spin faster but couldn't keep it up so eventually they stopped spinning. A matchbook cover popped open and a stack of photographs fluttered in the air, then settled in disarray.

We moved from the apartment on Franklin Avenue to a small house on De Longpre Street in Hollywood. It was November of 1964 and, as a number of people had become attached to us, we began forming a team. Several had artistic talents or possessed technical abilities, while others had publishing skills.

In December of that year, my wife held a Christmas party, and at the end of the evening, some of us were discussing the spinning sunglasses that I had told them about. Someone suggested that we mentally try to knock the balls off the Christmas tree. Singularly, no one could do it, so we began to pair up. Eventually I paired up with Kermit (a crop-dusting pilot), which did the trick. We selected a ball, concentrated on it, and sent it flying across the room! The shouts of amazement brought my wife into the room to scold and lecture us about wasting our precious psychic energy. Afterwards, we stood at the open door talking. (All the lights were out except one in the adjoining room.) Suddenly, a cutout of a flying saucer, made of heavy poster board, slid down the wall and hit the light switch, turning off the light.

The extraterrestrials informed us that this telepathic ability was passé, so it would be sacrificed for the sake of a more important talent – Zero-Zero-Telepathy. In the case of Copy and Cancel Telepathy, a part of the brain that, over the years, had become unhindered by the Frequency Barrier, is stimulated more than it had ever been by psychic energy. The rest of the brain is put into a state of low-powered stand-by. In other words, the telepathic area receives the most psychic energy, relative to the remainder of the brain which is in a state of mild hypnosis. When a person sleeps, they withdraw psychic energy from the brain and go into a state of mild hypnosis. This recession of psychic energy is called *de-trending*. Upon awakening, the brain is flooded with psychic energy. This reintroduction of psychic energy is called *ava-trending*. Most dreams are formed in isolated pockets that are receiving more psychic energy than the rest of the sleeping brain. For this reason, after awakening, many dreams cannot be remembered.

The extraterrestrials tell us that *the Universe is without and within us all.* This means that every galaxy, sun, planet and moon, as well as the personality of every person, exists within our individual psychic being (that is to say, all things). In Copy and Cancel Telepathy, communication must be conducted through the Universal Life Field over vast distances. This type of communication is costly in psychic energy. Zero-Zero telepathy is not very costly in psychic energy and, as a result, permits longer sessions and the transmission of more complex material and concepts.

15
The Mind Center

October 1992

In 1965, with the help of Lynn Gibbs, The MIND Research Foundation was formed. The foundation became headquartered on East Franklin Boulevard, in Hollywood, California (in the shadow of Griffith Park Observatory). The "Center" became beautiful as it began to be decorated by the MIND-staff artists, including art pieces and oil paintings depicting extraterrestrial spacecraft. Most of these oils were painted by Estelle Isigo, who was a Caucasian lady who chose to remain with her Japanese husband in an internment camp during World War II. Estelle authored a book describing her internment, entitled *Lonely Heart Mountain.* It was with great joy and satisfaction that I heard her personally thanked during the 1990 Academy Award Ceremonies for her contribution to an award-winning documentary based on her book.

The MIND staff was composed of many talented people. We began working together by producing a finely illustrated 35mm slide program with a soundtrack. This program was shown nightly (free of charge) to a standing-room-only crowd for nearly two years. Following these showings, I would finish with up-dated information along with earthquake predictions passed to us by the extraterrestrials and eventually noticed by the news media.

During the first few months of the Center's operation, I began to notice about six men in the audience who came early to get good seats and did not accept the free refreshments served at intermission. These men were similarly dressed, conspicuous with their short haircuts among the long-haired "Flower Children" of the time. One intermission I confronted the men, out of curiosity. Instantly, each held up his credentials as an agent of the Federal Bureau of Investigation (F.B.I.). They wouldn't tell me why they were there every night. For the next few months we reserved six seats for them with signs that read "Reserved for the F.B.I.," which made them much warmer towards us.

The Center was always filled to its 114-person capacity due to word-of-mouth and a simple ad that was placed in the *New Cosmic Star*, a New Age newspaper. The ad contained a drawing of a saucer-shaped spacecraft and the question, "Do you want to know the truth?" We also became involved in several call-in radio talk shows.

One day I received a call from television producer Gene Roddenberry, who told me he had heard of our slide presentations and lectures and requested permission for some of his writers to attend for a few nights. I told him it would be fine. We met later on two occasions and discussed what had become known as the Patrax Material. Mr. Roddenberry was happy to hear of the non-interference position of the Federation toward non-member cultures. This was later referred to as the "Prime Directive" on many *Star Trek* episodes.

As time went on, we began to publish a monthly mimeographed newsletter called *The Prism*, which contained articles pertaining to New Age subjects such as UFO sightings and associated earthquakes, extraterrestrial poetry, and other Patrax Material. *The Prism* eventually reached a circulation of about a thousand people.

UFO/Earthquake Connection

On March 9, 1966, on a radio show, I predicted that there would be earthquakes in China that would bring alien spacecraft to areas within the state of Michigan, when the station's engineer held a sign up to the studio window that read, "Keep it going. The quakes in China, and a story of UFO sightings in Ann Arbor, Michigan, are both coming over the wire as you talk." Matters became hectic several nights later as newspaper accounts told of hundreds of people seeing UFOs in the night sky over the Griffith Park Observatory (just a few blocks from the MIND Center). Those knowing of our location relative to the park were inquiring if we were in some way related to the UFOs. The head and first paragraph of two such articles were: "MYSTERIOUS PARK LIGHTS INVESTIGATED—The Air Force Thursday investigated numerous reports about two mysterious lights sighted over Griffith Park about 10 p.m. Wednesday," and "SKY LIGHTS MYSTIFY L.A.—The source of mysterious red lights in the sky over Los Angeles last night left numberless viewers puzzled today."

The radio show and local UFO sighting caused another TV producer to inquire if we (my wife, JoNell, and I) would like to be on a TV show hosted by attorney Melvin Belli. Mr. Belli was well known at the time as the flamboyant attorney of Jack Ruby, the assassin of Lee Harvey Oswald. I had witnessed this type of show before. The host asks questions and then chuckles with a raised eyebrow at every answer given by the guest, who comes away feeling like a fool or crackpot. I told the producer that I had a problem with doing the show, and he asked what it was. I told him I didn't feel that Mr. Belli was qualified to ask me questions. After a period of silence, he asked, "How does he become qualified?" Several days later, Melvin Belli was at the MIND Center. He absorbed every bit of the material in the slide program and all the information I was able to tell him.

We did four shows with Mr. Belli which were taped before a live audience, eight to ten days prior to airing on KTTV, Channel 11 in Los Angeles. The first two shows pertained to general Patrax Material such as the earthquake/UFO connection and what was known at the time about extraterrestrial spacecraft propulsion.

On the third Belli television show, I was prepared to make a number of earthquake predictions (which were passed on to me by extraterrestrials via telepathic communication). The show on which the predictions were made was taped on Sunday, May 29, 1966, and aired ten days later on June 8, 1966, at 10:30 p.m. I predicted sizable earthquakes for four areas within the next three weeks. The area with the greatest possibility of being first was located on the border of Chile and Peru. On June 7, 1966, the fault that runs through part of Chile and Peru generated an earthquake of considerable magnitude. The prediction also stated that if an earthquake occurred at this location, UFO sightings would take place within 72 hours in Texas, Colorado and Oklahoma. On June 7, 1966, blinking lights on a cylindrical shaped UFO were reported by citizens of Hartshorne, Oklahoma, who were Mrs. Altaclaire Morgan (wife of the town's postmaster), and Mr. Arlie Freeman, Chief of the Hartshorne Police.

A fourth Belli television show was taped and aired in July, 1966. On this show, Mrs. Morgan and Chief Freeman were interviewed over the telephone by Mr. Belli. Their accounts left no doubt that the UFO sightings and the earthquakes were related. Somehow I could foretell when an earthquake was going to occur and when and where the UFOs would be operating relative to a particular earthquake. After this show, there was quite a bit of flack from the scientific community (seismologists) who, in essence, stated that "they could not predict the time or place of an earthquake, therefore nobody else could." They were quieted when each of the remaining three predicted earthquakes took place within the three-week time frame included in the prediction. The days following the airing of the fourth Belli TV show brought waves of people to our door, causing us to close the Center and take a short vacation.

Patent Problems

People from all walks of life came to us because of the Belli shows. A couple who had seen my wife and me on the Belli shows, Rudy and Linda Stengle, began to visit the Center almost daily. Rudy was German-born, and the editor of *Design News*, a magazine that published information on everything that was newly invented and designs for every type of industry, from farming to nuclear power. His wife Linda was Canadian and an international journalist. She spoke with a slight European accent and mentioned several times that she had been on journalistic assignments in the Soviet Union. Linda was a personal friend and student of Stuart Robb, the well-known expert on the Quatrains of Nostradamus. Rudy entertained the staff many times by playing classical music on the organ. He also had a vast knowledge of physics and chemistry. I would say his IQ was that of a genius. It was a joke among the staff that "we had our own captured German scientist." Rudy's main interest was in the alien spacecraft propulsion system which had been lightly covered on the second Belli show. After looking at a detailed sketch I had made of the system, he proclaimed, "Do you know what you've got here? This is the answer that physicists are looking for, a physical means to contain high-temperature plasma. This is worth a lot of money. For 10% of the system, I will file a patent on it for you." I agreed that the patent would be filed by Entropy Limited, a Canadian company owned by Rudy and Linda and managed by Linda's son from a previous marriage.

I was soon informed by the Canadian Patent Office that I was deep in trouble, as I was in violation of the U.S. Atomic Energy Act of 1954. This act said that no U.S. citizen could file a patent on a nuclear device in a foreign country without first offering it to the U.S. Government. Lynn Gibbs came to my rescue by introducing me to John Newton, an Icelander who was a scientist at the famous "Kelly's Skunk Works." The Skunk Works worked on top-secret aircraft designs such as the U-2 spy plane. John, at the time, was also director of the prestigious "Leif Ericson Society" and convinced those of the U.S. government who were concerned about my attempt to file the patent in Canada that it was sincerely due to ignorance. Rudy also plead ignorance.

In the lull after the first patent fiasco, the MIND staff (in body) went to Reno, Nevada, to attend the UFO convention where we met Roland and Muriel West, owners of West Foods of Soquel, California, and Salem, Oregon. (At the time, West Foods was the second largest mushroom-grower in the world). During the convention, Reno had a power blackout that lasted several hours. The press picked up on the fact that the UFO convention was under way in town and that UFOs had been seen just prior to the great New York power blackout a year or so earlier. One impromptu speaker at the convention stated that he had seen a spacecraft land just outside the city limits, and "...a man got off the craft and spoke to him in German." The man who told this story was an employee of the power company and was out looking for the cause of the blackout.

During this convention, all of the airlines went on strike, leaving everyone stranded. We were able to get a few seats on a departing flight to Los Angeles for some of our staff and our daughter,Deanna. All flights thereafter were canceled. Our solution was to buy a used car. We bought a 1960 powder-blue Buick convertible from an Air Force officer and started for home. I received a telepathic message from the extraterrestrials that advised us to "by-pass Hollywood and drive to Lake Elsinore, California (inland and south of Los Angeles)." A few days later we were driving (top down, Kermit at the wheel) eastward over the mountains toward Lake Elsinore. It was a pleasant, sunny, summer afternoon.

Blinding Flash

Suddenly there was a blinding flash of white light that lasted about one second. My wife and I were bending down out of the air-stream to light cigarettes when the flash occurred. I felt a burning sensation on my forehead. I was surprised to see Kermit attempting to regain his sight. His skin was burned red and peeling off his face and eyelids. I had received my burn from the light reflecting off the chrome windshield wipers. As Kermit tried to control the car on the winding mountain road, the forest on both sides of the road burst into flames. Our lungs were burning and we gasped for nonexistent oxygen. Our only hope was to speed out of the area as fast as we could. An executive helicopter rose from the left side of the road and sped off. The pilot and passenger seemed to be suffering from the same problem.

Lake Elsinore had been a site for several pre-arranged spacecraft demonstrations. On several occasions a group of us would visit the area at night and watch three or four extraterrestrial spacecraft fly about over the lake, sometimes not more that a few feet off the water's surface.

The extraterrestrials told us telepathically that at the time of the blinding flash, one of their craft had landed in the nearby forest. The flash was that of an energy-emitting weapon that was fired at their spacecraft. The craft was hit and damaged. The crew managed to fly the craft to a remote gunnery range on the Camp Pendleton Marine Base near Oceanside, California, where they made repairs and left the Earth.

A few days later, there were new accounts of a flying object, thought to be an airplane on fire, flying over the Marine gunnery range. The extraterrestrials told us telepathically that the attack had come from another craft that had recently been constructed by surviving Nazi scientists in the Cordovan Mountains of South America. This was the craft seen in Reno with its German-speaking passenger, and also the craft responsible for the power blackout in New York City. The German-built aircraft (not capable of space flight) was required to recharge its propulsion system and weapon from electrical power lines, which then overloaded, causing equipment failures and blackouts. It was no coincidence that we were at the same place as the German saucer and the extraterrestrial spacecraft. The extraterrestrials informed us they knew the German craft would follow us from Reno. We were being used as bait!

UFO Attacked

The extraterrestrial craft was actually lying in ambush, but the Germans saw them first. The helicopter was traced to a steel company in the City of Industry, California. The owner of the company had recently been quoted in the news as being a believer in UFOs. When we called him, he refused to talk about the incident. Kermit's burns healed eventually, but the car was another story. Its once beautiful blue paint job would wipe off as a powder down to the metal. The top, upholstery, tires, and every rubber part deteriorated. No matter what was painted or replaced, the new parts also deteriorated, even brand new tires. We gave the car away.

During the time the MIND Center was in operation, I was able to pre-arrange at least 23 extraterrestrial spacecraft demonstrations. In some cases, Air Force officers (in civvies) were present. They, as well as we, took high-speed infra-red photos of the objects which were requested by the Air Force-sponsored Condon UFO Investigation Committee at the University of Colorado, at Boulder. Having receiving the photos, they promptly lost them!

After hearing of our patent problems, Roland and Muriel West joined us financially, and we re-filed the patent in the U.S. The device was classified secret. At the request of the Atomic Energy Commission (A.E.C.), a group of us visited the agency's headquarters in Germantown, Maryland. The A.E.C. scientists told us that they would rather work on the device we were proposing than on any plasma-containment device then being developed in the U.S. We left with the hope they could acquire funds to begin the project. The real result of this meeting was a disaster, which I will explain later.

Searching for Dr. Halsey

During this time I spoke with Michael Barton about the missing Halsey airplane (see article in September issue). One day a person gave me a 1948 issue (mint condition) of *Fate Magazine*. On the cover it said, "Was Abraham Lincoln a Mystic?" In the background behind Lincoln's picture were pictures of the pyramids of Giza in Egypt. Within a day or so after receiving this gift, Michael called to tell me that during our ill-fated Halsey expedition, his wife Violet had bought a 1948 copy of *Fate Magazine* in a used book store. Michael's copy of the magazine was identical to mine and also in mint condition. We hastily met, and Michael was first to realize that the name Abraham Lincoln had fourteen letters in it and recalled the extraterrestrial telepathic message given to us on the morning we left the search area. The message was, "Tell Michael that the mystery of the Halsey plane disappearance will be solved by the pyramids and the number 14." The fact that the pyramids were on the cover of the magazine urged us to study its contents thoroughly. For some reason we did this separately. One of the stories in the magazine pertained to Indian legends of the "Havamasumus," a race of tall white-skinned people who lived long ago in Death Valley and "flew about in the bellies of silver birds." I obtained a map of the Death Valley area and found that there was a mountain called Pyramid Peak. I also realized that if Dr. Halsey had changed his original course by 14 degrees to the southwest, that new course would have taken him directly over Pyramid Peak and Death Valley. Michael also began to talk about Pyramid Peak and Wiregrass Ridge in Nevada. We soon became aware that we were talking about two entirely different Pyramid Peaks. His peak was located directly south of Wiregrass Ridge in an area designated "Township 14" on his map. We decided to check out his area first.

Michael, my wife JoNell, my daughter Deanna and I went to Mesquite, Nevada, and rented a pick-up truck. After driving as close to Wiregrass Ridge as we could, Michael and I left the women and set out for the ridge. We had pre-arranged to communicate to each other by walkie-talkie every 30 minutes (to conserve the batteries). As Michael and I climbed the hill (out of sight of the women and the pick-up), Michael called my attention to his compass, which no longer pointed north, but southwest. Looking with binoculars to the south, Michael was the first to see an extraterrestrial spacecraft parked on the side of a mesa. The dull gun-metal grey craft looked like a 1956 Chevrolet hubcap. In the glasses, it was quite large. As I surveyed the vehicle, a hatch was raised, but no one emerged. When the time came to communicate with JoNell, we heard a very excited voice advise that she and Deanna had seen a spacecraft fly overhead and disappear over the hill. She was concerned that the craft's crew might not be friendly. Michael and I headed back as fast as we could, and when hills blocked sight of the spacecraft, I remarked, "For all I know, that craft is still parked on the mesa." Michael went about with his compass pinned to a piece of black velvet covering a square of poster board; the compass continued to point only to the southwest.

My wife inquired of the extraterrestrials, via telepathy, if they would bring the search of Dr. Halsey to an end, as she was becoming irritated about the time being devoted to the matter. Their telepathic reply was: "Go to Death Valley and locate some Indian petroglyphs in a small canyon. Within a ten-mile radius of these petroglyphs, you will see a glint of light on a hill. That light is reflecting off the wreckage of an airplane."

Plane and Eagle Found

We went to Death Valley (without Michael Barton). From the highway maintenance supervisor, we obtained the location of the petroglyphs. We drove west of the petroglyphs in the late afternoon and saw a hill sparkling with light. We stopped. Even our rugged station wagon could not get close to the area. We realized it would soon be dark and decided to wait until daybreak the next morning to hike to the area. One of the women noticed a large bird flopping about in the desert. We went to it and discovered it was a golden eagle. The bird allowed us to pick it up. We placed it in an empty ice chest, gave it some water and took 8mm movies of the eagle drinking.

We and the eagle spent a comfortable night in a motel in the small town of Shoshone. We named the eagle "Glint," because the glint on the hill caused us to stop, then spot the eagle in his dilemma. Because some of the people in our group had to work the next day, the hike was postponed until dawn on the next Saturday. When we arrived, we watched the rising sun's rays begin to reflect off what was once an airplane. While hiking up the hill, we found pieces of the plane which we hoped had come from Dr. Halsey's Tri-Pacer. Our hopes faded when we found a large radial engine, partially buried from impact. Strewn about were machine guns and machine gun bullets, some engraved "1943." It was apparent that we had found a downed military plane. We learned later that the plane was a Navy F4-U, reported missing during a training flight in 1943. We notified the sheriff's office of our find. The next day, the Los Angeles Times ran an article: "Hollywood Psychic Locates Long-Lost Plane."

Glint, the eagle, had recovered on water and chicken-feed and needed his freedom. He was very friendly, allowing us to spread his wings for photos. We called the California Fish and Game Department, hoping they would return him to Death Valley. However, they informed us that we had to return him to the exact spot where we had found him. They advised us that they didn't believe he came from Death Valley because no eagles live there, and that eagles obtain their moisture from their prey and never drink water straight. We hastily developed our film of the eagle drinking, as proof of what we said. JoNell started a telephone inquiry that ended when she reached the Secretary of the Interior. Glint was trussed up in canvas and on his way to the Los Angeles Zoo, accompanied by a very frightened warden who told us horror stories about how dangerous these creatures are. Later, one of the staff artists painted "Glint" on one of the propeller blades of the F4-U we had found. This prop was taken to the L.A. Zoo where it became Glint's perch.

Sometime later, I was holding on to my breakfast as Kermit flew me to the narrow canyons of Death Valley, searching areas that were within ten miles of the petroglyphs. We passed over the crashed F4-U and the Navy was painting it yellow (to indicate it is a known wreckage). We didn't find any other crashed planes, but our ground party did find an undamaged target drone, which also made the papers. The extraterrestrials responded telepathically: "We found an airplane for you. That will be enough for the time being. Tell Michael that the number 14 and the subject of pyramids will still solve this mystery."

The lease was up on the Franklin Center, so we looked for new headquarters. We found and rented the main mansion of three that were on the Hathaway Estate, located in the Silverlake District of Los Angeles, and built in the 1920's by the movie producer Henry Hathaway (*Birth of a Nation*). On 38 acres, the home contained nine bedrooms, a ballroom and a 15-car underground garage. All of the homes on the estate were destined to be razed and replaced by condominiums.

After moving to the new location, I received a letter from the United States Department of State. They were passing on to me an invitation from the Soviet Academy of Science to attend and lecture on high-temperature plasma containment at Novoseversk, Siberia, the following month. Somehow the Russians had learned of the extraterrestrial high-temperature plasma-containment device that was the subject of my "top secret" patent application. Within a few days, both the front and back gates of the estate were guarded by unmarked cars containing F.B.I. agents. They took the license number of each car that entered and exited.

Federal Agents' Accusations

One afternoon, two men came to the house and identified themselves as Federal Agents. They asked me if I was an agent working for the Soviet Union? I, of course, told them I wasn't. After a tour of the old mansion, they left. John Newton later told me that the U.S. government thought the plasma-containment device was a Russian idea. Furthermore they thought that the Russians had a problem with their idea, and were using me to pick the brains of American scientists in the hope of having the Americans solve the problem for them. They also thought that the invitation to the Soviet Union was a ploy to bring me to Russia for a debriefing.

In July, 1967, my wife and I were guests of Roland and Muriel West. My daughter Deanna was attending camp. The few members of the staff who lived at the center were present when two other members (who were not U.S. citizens at the time) were found removing records and recently taken UFO pictures from the center's office. They were held at gunpoint and then let go. Later on we returned home to find these items had indeed been taken in the burglary.

After the burglary, I was visited by Federal Agents who said I was an unregistered agent of a foreign power. When I asked, "What foreign power this time?" they replied, "The extraterrestrials." They said, "If you continue to speak publicly on the subject of UFOs, you and your wife will be arrested and taken someplace where you won't be any trouble to us. If you decide you want to be of help to your country, call this man." One of the agents handed me a business card that said "Mankind Research Unlimited, Mr. Schiliker." That night we held a telepathic session with the extraterrestrials. They advised us not to get involved with Mankind Research Unlimited, but to leave all behind and drop out of the public eye. The next day, we packed up our aged Mercury station wagon, said an emotional goodbye to the remaining staff and drove off.

My wife was very fearful of the government threats. We agreed to talk to others about what we had learned telepathically from the extraterrestrials only after we felt they could be trusted and were accepted as good people by the extraterrestrials. For the following 25 years we gathered as much extraterrestrial information as possible and even built devices that they inspired. We currently have a number of projects on the drawing board, so to speak. Descriptions of these projects will be the subject of future articles.

16

The Patrax Projects: Part 1

November 1992

Though I have telepathically communicated with extraterrestrials in the presence of people other than my family, (for Patrax Reasons), I have never done so in a public setting (other than at pre-arranged space-craft demonstrations). Nor have I ever had a extraterrestrial telepathic session that was initiated in order for another person to ask personal questions. Both, my extraterrestrial contacts and I, have refrained from using our telepathic relationship for anything other than to impart information that applies to everyone in general. If it had not been for this policy, my past twenty-eight years of telepathic activity in the Frequency Barrier would have taken it's toll, and I would be now long dead.

Since leaving the public scene in 1967, I have attempted to learn from the extraterrestrials whatever I could about anything they are aware of, that in turn, might help we of earth, have better lives. This twenty-five year activity became arranged into a list of "projects." Some of these extraterrestrial projects I totally understand, others, I have only enough understanding to speak of them in basic terms. The latter is due to the lack of specific telepathic references pertaining to the subject(s) that could develop these projects on their own or at least provide us with a different perspective. I think the following quote says what I'm trying to say quite well:

"Discovery consists of seeing what everybody has seen, and thinking what nobody has thought." Dr. Albert Szent-Gyorgyi.

The information contained in this article might really be only academic, as there is a strong possibility that the Frequency Barrier's demise will occur prior to any of the projects being finished. Thereafter, we will be able to physically associate with the extraterrestrials and benefit directly from their knowledge and technology. That is to say, such telepathically inspired projects could then be abandoned. Until the day comes when the Frequency Barrier is gone and we establish physical contact with the extraterrestrials, it might be wise to give the E.T. inspired projects some thought.

Universal Life Field Harmony

As mentioned in a previous article, the extraterrestrials have told us that they, as well as we, live and have our being in the Omni present, all permeating Universal Life Field (U.L.F.). Furthermore the E.T.'s have said that physical harmony with the U.L.F. death occurs (for any life form). Illness occurs (and can only occur) when one or more of a life form's biological systems has a weak relationship with the U.L.F. The importance of this extraterrestrial information is clear. If we can find means to maintain a strong relationship to the U.L.F., we are naturally bound to live a longer and healthier life. The extraterrestrials tell us that there are ways to maintain a strong physical relationship to the U.L.F. "The key is simply knowing what to·do and when to do it." The E.T.'s have also pointed out that there is a relationship between the U.L.F. and what we have come to call the three major "Natural Bio-Rhythms."

Bio-Rhythms and the U.L.F.

It is fairly well accepted that was as humans, physically, mentally, and emotionally function under the influences of three major bio-rhythms. These three bio-rhythm cycles take days to complete, before they begin again. It is apparent that during one-half of a bio-rhythm cycle, the particular faculty that pertains to the cycle gets progressively stronger (becomes more and more supportive). For the second half of either of the three bio-rhythms, the strength of the faculty progressively diminishes (becomes less and less supportive).

It has been determined that the physical bio-rhythm cycle takes 23 days to complete, the intellectual bio-rhythm cycle take 33 days, and the emotional bio-rhythm cycle takes 28 days. Although we are also influenced by bio-rhythm cycles that take only a 24 hour period to complete (Circadian cycles), and those that take less than 24 hours to complete (Ultra-danian cycles), the E.T.'s tell us to ignore them, along with the physical and intellectual cycles. The E.T.'s say that these cycles are "really under the control of the 28 day emotional cycle.

Those who use the knowledge of bio-rhythms in their daily lives have found the 28 day cycle to be the most reliable. The Japanese National Railroad Company for one, among many other types of industries throughout the world, give employees less responsibility during the down part of their 28 day bio-rhythm cycle. It has been found that this practice has reduced accidents considerably.

The U.L.F., 28 Day Bio-Rhythm, and the Neo-Natal Period

The human ingestion period is about 280 days, or ten 28 day cycles. The fact that some births occur earlier, and later, than 280 days, determines a person's future U.L.F. relationship. The closer the fetus comes to the 280 day gestation time before being born, the better off his or her later life will be relative to the U.L.F.

More infants die within the first 28 days after birth (Neo-Natal period) than at any other time (naturally) thereafter. The extraterrestrials tell us that a new-born must negotiate one full 28 cycle on it's own, during which it's internal organs and other biological systems attempt to relate to the U.L.F. If this biological harmony with the U.L.F. is accomplished, the infant's chances of living to adulthood are greatly increased.

The extraterrestrials say that a study of the causes of Neo-Natal infant death will provide us with very important information, which in turn can be used by us to obtain a greater harmonious relationship to the U.L.F. Such a study should reveal that during certain days, say for the sake of explanation that more infants die of heart failure during fourth to sixth day of the Neo-Natal period. This means that the biological function of the infant's heart did not harmonize (when it was supposed to in the cycle) with the U.L.F. Thus, the infant died of heart failure. In the same manner, it might be found than an infant's kidneys must harmoniously relate to the U.L.F.from the ninth to tenth day of the Neo-Natal Period. If the function of the kidneys does not harmonize with the U.L.F. during the ninth and tenth day of the period, the infant dies of kidney failure.

Knowing what organ, or biological system failed in infant death during what days of the 28 day Neo-Natal period informs us of the exact time during our own individual 28 day bio-rhythm cycle, when our heart, kidneys, or other biological systems are "Super Relating" to the U.L.F. Again, for the sake of explanation: Let's say it is determined when a particular organ or biological system is individually "Super Relating" to the U.L.F. We can do things to help the relationship become stronger. The term "Super Relating" means: the best degree of U.L.F. harmony the person's particular organ or biological system can achieve (under the person's present physical condition).

If we learn what organ or biological system is "Super Relating" to the U.L.F. and at what time in the 28 day bio-rhythm cycle, a person can regulate their nutritional requirements, or temporarily alter their life style in order to support the organ or the system's period of Super Relationship with the U.L.F. Every time one organ or biological system comes into greater harmony with the U.L.F., the other organs and systems of the body also improve (relatively) their harmony with the U.L.F.

It remains to acquire the references of the causes of Neo-Natal infant deaths. This information could be obtained from a computer study conducted in a Scandivanian country where each and every infant death is autopsyed. Only these references are acquired extraterrestrial telepathic assistance will expand our knowledge of this new understanding of life.

The information that follows under the headings "Biofeedback" and "Human Brain-waves" is presented in order to prepare the reader for a description of naturally produced ELF waves and their relationship to U.L.F. as well. An understanding of these subjects is necessary in order to understand the subject of Terra-Cyclic Meditation and how the practice of this type of meditation can assist in producing a stronger U.L.F. relationship. Terra-Cyclic Meditation will be described in Part 2 of this article.

Biofeedback

"Biofeedback Training" is the term for teaching a person to consciously control a particular physiological function of the body; such as blood pressure, heart beat rate, muscle tension and mental attitude (state of consciousness). Biofeedback employs electronic instruments which, by means of electrodes attached to the proper location on the body, pick-up the bioelectrical activity caused by a particular biological function and in turn converts it to some other sort of audio, or visual signal which is called the "feedback signal." While consciously controlling the feedback signal, the trainee eventually learns how to generate the right feeling(s) at will, and thus consciously control the biological function. When this is accomplished, the biofeedback instrument is eliminated.

Human Brain-waves

The human brain emits four distinct brain-wave patterns, which have been assigned the names of four letters in the Greek alphabet. They are: DELTA, THETA, ALPHA and BETA. See the following chart for frequency ranges.

normally unconscious		normally conscious	
DELTA	THETA	ALPHA	BETA
.02 3	7	13.5	27
HERTZ (cycles per second)			
major frequency bandsin the electroencephalographic (E.E.G.) record			

DELTA brain-waves are generated by a person when one is asleep, or unconscious. THETA brain-waves are also produced during sleep and in fact, have been linked to the state of dreaming. BETA brain-waves are generated when a person is totally conscious and aware of what is happening around them in the world. ALPHA brain-waves are generated while a person is awake, but is relaxed, passive, and in a meditative state of mind. Electroencephalograph (e.e.g.) research has established that a person engaged in meditation will generate a greater volume of Alpha waves than those of any other type. E.e.g. research has also established that a person will generate more Alpha waves of 10.6 Hz. than Alpha waves of any other frequency. It will be shown in Part 2 of this article that this dominant 10.6 Hz. factor (called the Alpha baseline frequency) is extremely important!

ELF Waves

In 1970, the extraterrestrials encouraged me to investigate the subject of biofeedback, specifically, Alpha brain-wave biofeedback. While exploring Alpha biofeedback training, I became aware of a scientific report authored by Drs. C. Polk and F. Fitchen of the University of Rhode Island.

The report entitled "The Schumann Resonances of the Earth-Ionosphere Cavity-Extremely Low Frequency Reception at Kingston, Rhode Island." The report can be found in the *Journal of Research of the National Bureau of Standards - D Radio Propagation* - Vol.66D, No. 3, May-June, 1962. This paper describes the instrumentation that was used to receive and record the resonances and additionally describes the phenomenon as extremely low frequency electromagnetic wave-trains that are composed of individual wave cycles that are somewhat sinusoidal in shape.

These wave-trains which are products of lightning strokes occur naturally throughout the world, and are contained within a natural resonance cavity (wave-guide), composed of the Earth's surface and it's ionosphere. The natural resonance cavity that contain wave-trains is similar to the resonance chamber of a guitar or violin.

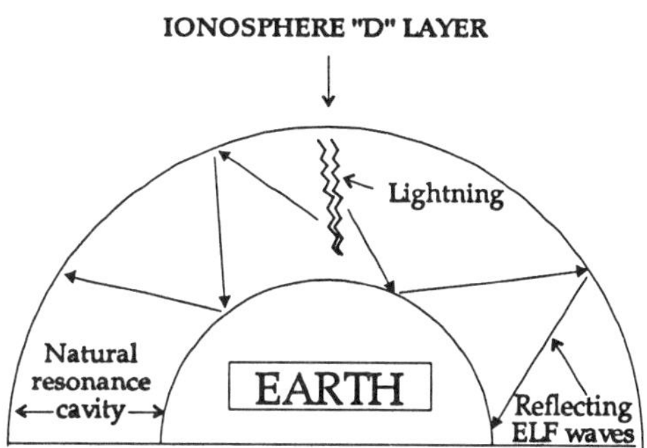

The existence of this phenomenon was first suggested by Dr. W. O. Schumann. Later working with Dr. H. Konig in Germany, Dr. Schumann constructed equipment that was used to record and verify the existence of the resonance phenomenon.

Drs. Schumann and Konig named these wave-trains Elf-waves. E-L-F meaning Extremely Low Frequency.

The earliest Elf-wave researchers determined that the average frequency range of the waves were 7 to 13.5 Hz. (cycles per second) and that wave-trains of 10.6 Hz. occur most frequently.

At this point it should be understood that the earliest Elf-wave frequency range data was obtained under adverse environmental conditions and because of insufficient electronic technology of the time exact data was not as refined as it is today and it is stated on page 12, paragraph 3 of the Polk-Fitchen Report, that researchers found it necessary to record Elf-waves at a location considered to be electromagnetically "quiet" (at least 1200 feet from a power line).

In 1970, 1976, 1979, and 1991, a group of associates and I, constructed progressively improved solid state Elf-wave filter amplifier, which now allows us to pick-up and record Elf-waves at any geographical location, even within buildings.

These solid state filter amplifiers allowed us to determine the following facts about the Elf-waves frequency range: Elf-waves frequency extends from .02 Hz. to 13.5 Hz. (first ceiling frequency). On rare occasions, frequencies above 13.5 Hz. are detectable. Frequencies of 7 to 13.5 Hz. occur more than any other, and wave-trains of 10.6 Hz. occur most frequently.

The Elf Wave-human Brain Wave Connection

As I stated, I was attracted to the Elf-wave phenomenon during my Alpha biofeedback research because I realized that Elf-waves and human brain-waves have the same frequency.

In fact, at most times, Elf-waves are occurring in the "Natural Resonance Cavity" that bracket the Alpha brain-wave frequency range, (7 to 13.5 Hz.).

Even more astonishing is that Elf-waves of 10.6 Hz. occur more than any other because 10.6 Hz. is also the frequency of the Alpha Wave most frequently generated by a meditating human being (the Alpha baseline frequency). Elf-waves and Alpha brain-waves are also similar as to their

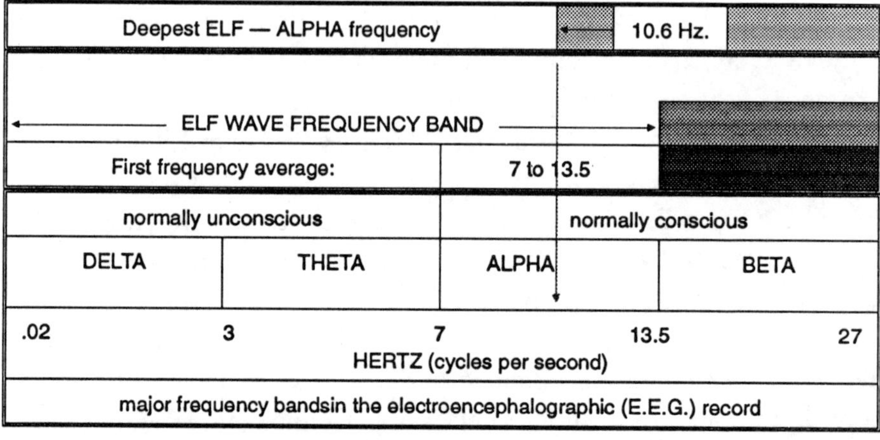

shapes (envelopes).

These similarities that exist between Elf-waves and human brain-waves in the form of their frequency averages and wave shapes; are impossible to dismiss as mere coincidence.

Experts in the field of electroencephalography (e.e.g.), unfamiliar with the existence of the Elf-wave phenomenon, have erroneously identified chart recordings of Elf-waves as being records of human brain-waves.

Part 2 of this article will describe the Terra-Cyclic Meditation and other projects inspired by the extraterrestrials.

17

The Patrax Projects: Part 2

December 1992

In Part 1 of this article, it was explained that lightening strokes occurring throughout the world generate electromagnetic waves, and because these wave-trains are of extremely low frequency (E-L-F waves) also described in Part 1 that Elf-waves have the same frequencies as the brain-waves that are produced by humans. It was also pointed out in Part 1 that Elf-waves with frequencies that are identical to the Alpha brainwave pattern of a human being occur more frequently, and that the most frequently occurring Elf-waves and Alpha waves have the same frequency which is 10.6 cycles per second (Hz.).

The first ceiling frequency of the Elf-wave phenomenon is 13.5 Hz. This is also the last frequency associated with the Alpha brain-wave pattern of humans. When the ELF/Alpha base line frequency of 10.6 Hz. is divided by 13.5 Hz. the result is .785185185...which is near the value of 1/4 Pi (.7853981634+). Because we are dealing with frequency, we are also dealing with time (cycles per standard second). This value for 1/4 Pi became more accurate when it is considered in the light of a "natural second of time" (about 1/5000 of a standard second longer in duration). For more information pertaining to "natural second of time," see my three book series The Rods of Amon Ra.

Pi (3.141592654+) is both an irrational number (can't be written as a common fraction), and a transcendental number (out of the field of perception by the senses). When 13.5 Hz. (first Elf/Alpha wave ceiling frequency) is multiplied by 12, the result is 162. Written as 1.62, which is very close in value to 1.618033989, known to present day mathematicians as Phi (ϕ). Phi is found in the proportional shape of everything around us, even ourselves.

The extraterrestrials tell us that the Phi is the creative number of EL's (Lord Gods) and that the infinite value of Pi is the creative number of "God the Creator of All Things This tells us that our bodies are proportioned on the creative number of the El's (Phi), and our brain functions are regulated by the incommensurable creative number of the Creator.

The extraterrestrials tell us that because our brains (and theirs) function in relation to the value of 1/4 Pi, we are therefore capable of intelligent thought. At the time a person attains the "infinite thought" (see earlier articles) and therefore becomes re-perfected, their consciousness joins with the consciousness of the Supreme Creator and operates with the full infinite value of Pi.

The extraterrestrials have informed us that we can employ lightning generated Elf-waves to gain stronger relationship to the Universal Life Field (U.L.F., see first part of this article). They tell us we can employ the naturally produced Elf-waves in the practice of "Terra-Cyclic Meditation" (Earth-Cycles). Before Terra-Cyclic Meditation is described, it is first necessary to understand the natural law of "Sympathetic Resonance

Law Of Sympathetic Resonance

The *Acker Encyclopedia of Physical Science* give the following definition for the Law of Sympathetic Resonance: "The reinforcement of the natural vibration of a system, or object by a force acting with the same frequency as the system. Every object, or system has a natural frequency or a frequency at which it will vibrate if displaced, or distorted, and then released.

A child on a swing (subject to the earth's gravity) is such a system. Once the swing is pushed, it tends to vibrate at it's natural frequency. If it is pushed lightly at intervals equal to that frequency, the displacement of the swing (how high it goes), increases rapidly. Theoretically, the displacement of any resonant system rapidly approaches infinity (unless friction or another dampening force acts upon it).

The natural frequency of an electrical oscillator circuit can be changed by adjusting the capacitance, or inductance in the circuit, and a radio station can be "tuned in" by adjusting the capacitance of the receiver to resonate at the frequency of the electromagnetic waves from the broadcasting station.

If the frequency of a light-wave matches some natural frequency of an atom's electrical charges, the wave is absorbed by the atom. Thus, atoms of gas in the sun's atmosphere absorb light of just those frequencies that correspond to the resonant frequencies of the atoms and this absorption produces the dark Fraunhofer lines which are seen in the solar spectrum

A reader what has access to a piano, can witness the Law of Sympathetic Resonance in action, by striking a "C" note on the keyboard and then observing how the other "C" strings of the instrument resonate sympathetically. The principle of resonance applies to all vibrating bodies that send out energy in waves, such as the human brain.

The similarities that exist between lightning generated Elf-waves and human brain-wave emissions suggest that human brain activity can be naturally stimulated by the continuously occurring Elf-waves, via the "Law of Sympathetic Resonance

This harmonic idea suggests that the human brain further consists of four resonant systems; which would be Delta, Theta, Alpha and Beta systems, and that the brain-wave frequencies that are generated by either of the four systems could be sympathetically reinforced by externally produced waves of similar frequencies.

In order to determine if Elf-waves do effect human e.e.g. activity naturally or could be made to influence it. A group of associates and I conducted the following experiment in 1972:

A subject trained to generate Alpha brain-waves at will, was attached to an Autogen 120 e.e.g. biofeedback instrument and asked to generate a continuous flow of Alpha brain-waves (7-13.5 Hz.). This he did, to the best of his ability.

The biofeedback instrument was set to filter out all brain-wave frequencies below 7 Hz. and above 14 Hz.

The Alpha waves generated by the subject were then recorded on a chart recorder and observed as well, on the first trace of a dual-trace oscilloscope.

The naturally produced Elf-waves that were occurring at the time, were fed into a "binary input" feature of the chart recorder and also observed on the second trace of the dual-trace oscilloscope. We were then able to observe the subject's Alpha brain-wave output and the then occurring Elf-waves on the scope simultaneously.

The binary input of the recorder activated a pen that marked a straight line on the border of the chart. When, and if, the subject's brain activity and the Elf-wave activity of the time matched perfectly, both in frequency and amplitude (intensity). This is similar to comparing a person's voice print, or a signature facsimile.

The room was silent, suddenly, the silence was broken by the sound of a solenoid that activated the binary input pen on the chart recorder. The click of the pen solenoid repeated again and again as it continuously turned off and on. These occurrences indicated that the external, lightning produced Elf-waves can in fact become integrated into the e.e.g. activity of a human being, by consciously preparing the proper mental state that is compatible to the frequencies of the Elf-waves (similar to tuning in the frequency of a radio station).

At that point in the experiment, those in observance could no longer contain themselves, and began to talk about the discovery. The excitement brought the test subject out of the Alpha-State of consciousness and into the Beta-State. Only then, did the sound from the pen solenoid stop.

Also, at this point, the subject arose from his chair and walked approximately 10 ft. to the Elf-wave pick-up coil (while still attached to the biofeedback unit). He then placed his hands about 6 in. from the coil and took several deep breaths. When he did this, the pen on the recorder which was still inscribing his brain-waves (in this case, Beta waves) went off the chart.

When the subject was asked to do it again, he couldn't. When he was asked why he did it in the first place? He replied: "I moved entirely on impulse

Because a person who is in meditation generates more Alpha type brain-waves than any other, and Elf-waves with the same frequency as the Alpha brain-waves, occur more often than any other. It came to me that the naturally occurring Elf-waves might be used to induce a state of tranquil meditation, that could eliminate stress. To accomplish this I turned to another phenomenon which is known as: "Evoked Potentials of Light

When a person who is attached to an e.e.g., visually experiences a flash of light, after a few milli-seconds (thousandths of a second) a spike will appear on the graph. This spike represents a bioelectrical event that took place in the person's brain, which was caused by a photonic energy in the light flash. Photonic energy is electro-magnetic in nature.

The bioelectrical event that occurs in the brain düe to a flash of light, is called, an Evoked Potential Light.

Dr. Ertl of Denver, Colorado, uses Evoked Potential Light to determine a person's Intelligent Quotient (I.Q). He does this by measuring the time lapse between the light flash and the appearance of the spike on the e.e.g. Ertl says: "The faster the appearance of the spike on the graph, the higher is a person's I.Q

Terra-cyclic Meditation

In 1979, I obtained an "electronic shutter" (P.L.T.Z. ceramic) that permitted Elf-waves to be translated into analogous pulses of light, that is, one pulse per 1/2 wave cycle. The shutter's aperture (degree of openness) was electronically set to respond to the amplitude (intensity) of any particular Elf-wave cycle occurring at the time. Therefore, the pulsing light increases, or decreases in brightness relative to the various amplitudes of the cycles that compose any naturally occurring Elf-wave train.

Photographic images (or just a white light) were then projected from a slide projector through the shutter and therefore the projected image was able to be pulsed on and off the viewing screen as the same frequency and amplitude (brightness) as the then occurring Elf-waves. In turn, "Evoked Potentials of Light" were able to be induced in all observers via the light pulse, at the same time frequency and amplitude of the then occurring Elf-waves.

In 1977, the Elf instrument (as it was called at the time) was set up in a mobile home on the grounds of the Santa Maria Health Resort and Clinic, located between Tiajuana and Ensenada, Mexico. The Elf-waves occurring at the time were in the form of light pulses projected into a boxlike slide viewer. The screen of the viewer was about 8 inches high by about 12 inches wide. We left the instrument operating and went for coffee at the resort's restaurant which was directly across the street. We left behind the middle-aged woman who occupied herself with knitting as she took care of some children. About 20 minutes later, the woman ran into the restaurant very excited. She related that she had been for deaf in her left ear for years, and had been steadily losing her hearing in her right ear. She went on to say that as she knitted, she became relaxed due to the pulsing light (Elf-waves). She then heard a loud "crackling sound) in here deaf left ear, thereafter the hearing in that ear was fully restored and the hearing in her right ear greatly improved. Because we were not recording the waves and the time, we had no idea what pattern of Elf-waves brought about her cure.

After this miraculous event, the method of presenting "Elf pulsed" images was up-dated, when a colored television set was modified to "Elf pulse" video taped material, along with soothing music, or sound effects. Nature scenes and sounds are very pleasing to experience in this manner.

The system came to be called "The Terra-cyclic Mediational Aid and Stress Reducer The Terra-Cyclic system has done everything that was ever expected of it and more. For example: phenomenal effects, both temporary and long lasting, in the area of extra-sensory perception have been observed.

The Terra-Cyclic Mediational aid is being considered as a nutrition, and medication enhancer. The most recent updated version of this instrument is equipped with out-put jacks for electronic "Elf Wave Acupuncture. This allows a person not only to meditate with the Elf-waves in the form of light pulses, but also receive appropriate acupuncture treatments with the very same Elf-waves they are physically viewing. It is hoped that this body/brain stimulus will be more effective in bringing about cures for such things as drug addiction. When the Neo-Natal Infant Death study was, described in Part 1 of this article, is conducted, and the knowledge of which organ or biological system is Super Relating during what time of day the 28 day bio-rhythm cycle, Elf-wave Acupuncture can be employed to assist that particular organ or system Super Relate to a greater degree than it did since and earlier time in the person's lifetime. The same knowledge can also be used to determine the best times for organ transplants, as it will in some cases help retard bio-logical rejection.

It is my hope to make the Terra-Cyclic Mediational Instrument available in a church like setting, free of charge. Hopefully, this type of setting will protect it from those that prefer that it wouldn't exist. Elf-waves acupuncture might also become available, but such treatments can only be carried on by a state licensed acupuncturist.

Part 3 of the article will pertain to such extraterrestrial inspired things as Deuterium Free water.

18
The Patrax Projects: Part 3

January 1993

Once I asked the extraterrestrials how long they lived, expecting an answer of about 200 to 300 years. I was overwhelmed to hear them reply that they could live as long as 5,000 to 50,000 years, depending on the world they came from and their present level of personal spiritual development. I then asked why we of Earth age and die so rapidly, relative to their life spans. They responded, "Aging on Earth is really a disease brought on by the fact that the water on the earth contains a toxic substance called deuterium."

Deuterium is an isotope of the element hydrogen. Hydrogen has two known isotopes, deuterium and tritium. Hydrogen is composed of one positively charged proton (+) and one negatively charged electron (-); deuterium has the same particle composition but has an additional particle in its nucleus called a neutron that has no charge. For approximately every 6,700 atoms of hydrogen found in water, there is one deuterium atom. Tritium has one proton, one electron and two neutrons in its structure. Tritium is rarely found in nature, but can be manufactured.

Heavy Water

Deuterium or tritium as isotopes of hydrogen can replace hydrogen in any chemical compound. One molecule of atomically pure water is composed of two hydrogen and one oxygen atom (H_2O). Deuterium is heavier than hydrogen due to the additional weight of the neutron it contains in its nucleus. If deuterium replaces the hydrogen in the water molecule the result is called heavy water (D_2O).

Most people are familiar with the heavy water being used in the field of nuclear physics. In fact, it is used along with lead as radiation shielding around a nuclear reactor because it absorbs radiation.

The extraterrestrials point out that old age and radiation poisoning (radiation sickness) have the same symptoms. Some of them are lack of pigmentation (especially in hair), sterility, and the gradual deterioration of the circulatory system. The ETs say that the deuterium in our bodies, which we have accumulated over our lifetimes from ingesting the toxic water of the Earth, absorbs and retains radiation from the sun and other environmental sources. Therefore, we age due to the biological disruption brought about by radiation damage. This radiation damage would not occur as severely as it does if we had no deuterium (or less deuterium) in our bodies. Deuterium does its biological damage on the cellular level. The DNA molecule in each of us is different; it contains every characteristic of our individual biological makeup.

The DNA molecule is in the form of a double helix. The two parts of the helix are formed on both sides of peptide bonds composed of hydrogen. These hydrogen bonds are like rungs in a ladder and easily break apart to allow the cell to replicate (reproduce itself). As time goes on, deuterium begins to replace hydrogen in the DNA peptide bonds. These bonds, composed to some degree of deuterium, do not break apart as easily as those composed of pure hydrogen. Eventually, the stronger bonds do break apart, but not before the cell has been subjected to radiation in degrees beyond its natural tolerance. The replicated cell therefore makes an inferior copy of itself; thereafter, each generation of cells becomes more and more inferior. When the cells are no longer able to replicate, they can no longer relate in any degree of harmony with the Universal Life Field (U.L.F.) and the person simply dies of old age.

When a person is born, the cells of the body contain a 7.7 multi-millivolt electrical charge. By the age of 65, a person's cells have only a .7 multi-millivolt charge. Accumulating deuterium in the cells of the body absorbs radiation that in turn progressively robs the cells of their normal electrical potentials. The combined electrical potential of all the cells of our bodies provides (like little electrical storage batteries) the bioelectrical power we use to think and to stimulate such things as our heart muscles. Lack of enough electrical power from the cells to operate our brain functions results in diseases such as Alzheimer's.

We are made of about 72% water. Over the years, the atomically pure water present in our cell, at birth progressively becomes replaced by toxic heavy water. A research project carried out at my request by a company that supplies deuterium for scientific experimentation found that the older we get, the more deuterium is present in our blood. The cost of testing each of the test subject's blood was $250.

A Membrane Would Filter Toxins

When a fetus is developing, the placenta filters out any deuterium that might reach the fetus via the mother's blood stream. Imagine how rapidly the cells of a fetus replicate. Therefore, a manufactured substance that can act similar to a placenta (a membrane) might be developed to filter deuterium from hydrogen during the process of electrolysis. The pure hydrogen obtained from this process can be chemically united with oxygen to form molecules of atomically pure water. Consequently, no such artificial membrane exists that would allow the smaller hydrogen atoms to pass through while preventing the larger deuterium atoms from passing through.

Deuterium is produced by using evaporation and a considerable amount of electricity. A gram of deuterium acquired by this process currently costs about $450. The cost of getting all of the deuterium out of a considerable volume of water is great. In 1987, I encouraged the same company mentioned earlier to produce atomically pure water. They called it "light water." They produced 110 gallons of light water at a cost of $1,000 per gallon. This, needless to say, I could not afford to buy from them.

The company also provided me with research that had been carried out concerning the toxicity of deuterium in the body. Among the data was a case of a physicist who attempted to murder his wife by giving her nothing but heavy water to drink. Though she detected no difference in the water, her rapid aging gave away the murder plan.

In the republic of Georgia, a member of the recently formed Federation of Russian Republics, is found a group of people, the Hunsas, who are famous for living for well over 100 years. It is reported that the men of this group are able to father children even after they reach an advanced age. The question is, what is the great secret of Hunsa longevity? The answer is the water they drink. They obtain their water from ancient mountain glaciers that contains very little deuterium. These glaciers reflect a certain shade of blue (not exactly the color of the sky). This unique color corresponds to the color (wavelength) of a spectral line that is emitted or absorbed by deuterium when the atom is energetically excited. This wavelength is reflected because there is little or no deuterium in the glacier ice to absorb it. Peruvian Indians living in high elevations also obtain their drinking water from glacial ice. Some of these Indians also live to be well over 100 years old. Recently, I heard of a woman from this area, who is believed to be 145 years old. The extraterrestrials tell us that the reason for this longevity is due to "not what's in the water, but what's not in the water."

It did not surprise me to learn that, cocktail bars in Japan are charging $2 extra for a cocktail that contains ice cubes made from water from glacial ice.

A recent television documentary pointed out that water companies such as Perrier that obtain their water from deep artesian wells were concerned because they had been observing a marked increase in contaminants (among them deuterium) following atmospheric nuclear tests conducted somewhere on the planet.

The extraterrestrials tell us that the Earth's water became contaminated when the planet Maldec exploded many years ago. It was explained in an earlier article how this event caused the Frequency Barrier to begin on Earth. The extraterrestrials tell us that a by-product of this explosion was a vast cloud of deuterium gas. Four years after this cataclysmic event, the Earth passed through this cosmic cloud of deuterium. The Earth, prior to this, had had a very rich atmosphere of oxygen. Electrical storms that occurred combined the Earth's oxygen with the deuterium in the cosmic cloud, causing it to rain heavy water, which mixed with the waters of Earth.

Is it not a curious thing? The Biblical patriarchs such as Methuselah lived as long as 900 years, but after the Great Flood, we began to live shorter and shorter lives.

Polar Ice is Deuterium-Free

The extraterrestrials tell us that the ancient polar ice that was formed prior to the explosion of Maldec is deuterium-free. But water from such ice should be both distilled and sterilized. The reason they gave for the need for sterilization is that the ancient bacteria (frozen in suspended animation) can be activated and cause a health threat to the Earth's human, plant and animal life, which is no longer immune to certain strains of these ancient bacteria.

The element hydrogen has a natural resonant frequency of about 1,420,405,752.7 Hz. It is possible that using the natural Law of Sympathetic Resonance, this frequency might be used to separate deuterium from our water supplies. Thereafter, we could provide atomically pure water not only for ourselves, but for our livestock, too. Hydroponic farming will certainly be the wave of the future. The extraterrestrials tell us that when we stop ingesting deuterium contaminated (toxic) water, the pituitary gland, which identifies the amount of water the body needs, will eventually become purged of what is called deuterium addiction. When this purge is accomplished rejuvenation will occur, as the body's only source of water would then be atomically pure water.

In the 1970's, the subject of "Pyramid Power" was very much the rage. It was found by those who researched the subject that meat and vegetables left for a period of time in a hollow pyramid (a scaled down version of the Great Pyramid of Giza), the material lost 66% of its water. Does anyone want to bet that the 44% of the water left behind in the material was heavy water?

Another possibility pertaining to the removal of deuterium from our water is a device that was also inspired by the extraterrestrials. It is called the "Molecular Resonator" (see my three-book series, *The Rods of Amon Ra*).

Hopefully, in the near future, there will be an abundant amount of atomically pure water (deuterium-free) for everyone, and not just for the establishment's privileged. When that day comes, let me drink deeply to your health, with the toast, "May the force be with you always, and may you live long and prosper."

19
The Patrax Projects: Part 4

February 1993

Having questions about so-called incurable diseases, we wondered whether or not diseases such as cancer or AIDS were affected by the Frequency Barrier. If not, could the extraterrestrials provide us with a way to do away with such afflictions? This article presents the extraterrestrial response to these questions.

The extraterrestrials tell us that there is a pre-Frequency Barrier DNA in microbes that are frozen deep in the Earth's polar ice caps. These microbes are in a state of suspended animation. When they are revived, biologists should find successive generations interesting to study. Once the ancient microbes are revived from their present state of suspended animation, they will be subjected to the mutating effects of the Frequency Barrier. Biological changes will take place in the microbes and over a period of time will provide Earth scientists with invaluable data.

The Body as a Biochemical Factory

When the extraterrestrials were asked telepathically how they dealt with bacteria and viral infections of the body, they replied, "We employ psychopharmaceutics. That is to say, we formulate specific antibacterial and antiviral chemistry by stimulating the brain with light-coded information that first tells the brain what the body is infected with and then evokes subtle mental commands to all glands to produce or contribute to a biological formula that attacks the particular infection. The human body is the best biochemical factory in existence.

Stimulating the human brain into action against any form of infection is difficult to do naturally on Earth due to the restricting effects of the Frequency Barrier. However, the restrictions can be overcome by the use of a fantastic instrument called a rhythmetacator. In order to understand how the rhythmetacator works, it is first important to understand the following: (1) The formulation of the related keys and (2) the galvanic skin response (G.S.R.) in relation to hypnosis.

Formulation of the Related Keys

In order to determine what color pattern of lights (related key) will stimulate the brain to take defensive biological action against an infecting microbe or virus, several things must be done: (1) A sample of the microbe or virus must be cultured in a nutrient that encourages reproduction. (2) The colony, along with its sustaining nutrients, is subjected to a measured amount of electricity and vaporized. (3) The vaporization event is photographed with a transparency film in a camera attached to a spectroscope. A spectroscope allows the spectral lines of any element present in the nutrient and microbe or virus to be identified and thus photographed as a record. In the case of a microbe or virus and its nutrient, the resulting photograph will reveal a body of blended colors (wavelengths). The body of blended colors is called a band spectrum. (4) A sample of the microbe or virus growth medium (nutrient) is then vaporized without the presence of any microbe or virus. This event is also photographed through a spectroscope. The result will be two color transparencies. One transparency will contain the band spectrum of the molecules that compose only the nutrient. (5) The transparencies are then inserted at opposing positions in an instrument called an interferometer. Both transparencies are projected into the instrument. The two sources of light that are used to produce the projections must be of the same intensity and be monochromatic (containing all wavelengths of the visible spectrum). The colors (band-spectrum wavelengths) that were recorded on the transparencies encounter each other in the interferometer. Those wavelengths that are of the nutrient will interfere only with the identical wavelengths of the nutrient that the microbe or virus once lived in prior to vaporization. After band spectrums of the nutrient recorded on both transparencies blend (due to identical wave reinforcement), the remaining colors (wavelengths) that do not reinforce each other are related only to the molecules that once made up the living microbe or virus.

The extraterrestrials tell us that there will be no more than twelve wavelengths (colors) that are related to any microbe or virus. The wavelengths will be different for each type of microbe or virus. Thus the wavelengths of light that relate to each and every microbe or virus must be identified by the means described above and recorded for any future l use. The related key pattern actually represents the molecular bridges that connect the organism to food. When these bridges are weakened, the organism either starves to death or fails to reproduce before natural death. The related key for any microbe or virus can be translated into a bar code of the type that is electronically scanned for product and price identification at supermarket checkout counters.

After the related key of an infectious microbe or virus is identified and bar-coded, the bar-coded information regarding the key is inserted into the Rhythmetacator.

The Rhythmetacator

The rhythmetacator is composed of eight components: (1) micro-computer; (2) related key formulator; (3) monochromatic light source; (4) fiberoptic transmission lines; (5) natural ELF-wave pickup coil and filter/amplifier; (6) artificial ELF-wave generator and frequency counter; (7) ponder scope; (8) galvanic skin response sensor.

When the bar code of a microbe or virus is inserted in to the rhythmetacator, a microcomputer reads the information and sends instructions to a unit called the related key formulator. The formulator scans the field of a spectrum that was derived from a monochromatic source of light (containing all visible wavelengths of light). After finding the wavelengths of the desired related key, the formulator then situates the ends of fiberoptic lines in such a way that they correspond to the sources of one to twelve possible colored lights that represent the related key of that particular microbe or virus. The formulator also dictates the intensity of each of the light sources (in some cases, not all wavelengths should be transmitted at the same intensity). The opposite ends of the fiberoptic transmission lines terminate in a viewing device called a ponder scope.

The ponder scope has two viewing areas, one for the right eye and one for the left. Each viewing area contains the ends of twelve fiberoptic lines. The fiberoptic terminals found in the center of the array are called the ELF marker terminals.

When the related key of a microbe or virus is being transmitted through the fiberoptics, the lights flash on and off at a predetermined frequency. The rate of flash is produced by an electronic frequency generator or is regulated by the waveform characteristics of the natural ELF waves that are produced by lightning. In most cases, the ELF marker lights would be white (all visible wavelengths), the marker flash rate and light intensity of the then-occurring natural ELF waves.

Coma and IQ Can Be Affected

The ELF marker system is really composed of the same instrumentation that is used in the Terracyclic Meditational Aid and Stress Reducer (described in my article in the December issue). ELF marker flashes based on naturally produced ELF waves can be used to mentally stimulate (through the eyelids) the brains of some persons who are in coma. Depending on the reason for coma, this activity over a period of time can bring the patient back to consciousness.

The right side of the human brain deals with abstract thought and controls the left side of the body. The left side of the brain deals with logical thought and controls the right side of the body. For this reason the rhythmetacator is equipped with visual deprivers. A visual depriver blocks the view of either the left or right related key arrays that are functioning at the time in the ponder scope. This permits only one hemisphere or the other of the brain to receive the influences of the related key. Optical illusions or pages of written text printed on transparencies backed by the flashing white marker lights, seen by both eyes or by either eye individually, can help increase memory and raise the IQ.

Explanation

Let's say a person is infected with tuberculosis (TB). The bar code for the TB germ is inserted into the rhythmetacator. The instrument automatically sets itself up to generate the related key of the TB microbe. The infected person then peers into the ponder scope at the flashing colors (wavelengths) of the related key. The period of observation is also predetermined and is called the ponder sequence. The person is also attached to an electrode sensor that responds to galvanic changes in the skin.

During the observance of the flashing related key, the person's brain begins to get bored with repetition. The brain will naturally retaliate with whatever it can. It will secrete biological material into the blood stream and command various glands to produce biological material. The biological material, individually or combined from all production sources, is, of course, deadly to any TB microbes in the body. In other words, the "pill" was mixed in the person's head. As mentioned before, internal formulation of specific substances that are in turn specially antibiological to a certain microbe or virus is called the practice of psychopharmaceutics.

When the bored brain sends out its signals and commands for antibiological production, the mental events become evident through changes that take place in the skin. The mental events are emotional in nature and affect the electrical conductivity of the skin. The measurement of skin conductivity is used in polygraphs (lie detectors). When the infected person's brain activity (related to the production of antibiological chemistry) causes changes in his/her skin, the change is noted by a pick-up electrode. An electronic command, via the electrode, is sent to the monochromatic light source in the related key formulator. The command causes the light in the formulator to become brighter to some degree. This increased light intensity (action) causes the brain to again or continuously respond in an adversarial biological manner.

The extraterrestrials tell us that no one should be subjected to a ponder sequence for longer than 15 minutes. If there was no galvanic skin response during a particular ponder sequence, the session should be terminated and the procedure carried out again at a later time.

A rhythmetacator treatment is best carried out during the peak 14 days of the person's 28-day biorhythm cycle. A rhythmetacator session can irritate a person who has a short attention span. But luckily such persons make good hypnotic subjects. The benefits of a rhythmetacator treatment will not be diminished even if the subject is to some degree under the influence of hypnosis or hypnotic suggestion.

Color-aided Acupuncture

The extraterrestrials tell us that there is a relationship between color and the acupuncture meridians. The acupuncturist places acupuncture needles into a particular meridian(s) in order to beneficially affect certain organs or physiological systems of the body. The color that is related to a particular acupuncture meridian or colors that individually relate to all other acupuncture meridians can be determined in the following way: A subject is placed under the influence of hypnosis. A needle is placed deep into the meridian. The subject is told that she or he will not feel any pain whatsoever and that every color of the visible spectrum will be passed before his/her eyes. Only one particular color (wavelength) will permit him/her to feel the presence of the needle.

G.S.R. Indicates Meridian's Color

The hypnosis subject is also attached to a galvanic skin response unit, so that when the subject sees the color that permits the needle to be felt, the feeling causes a change in the subject's skin conductivity. The color that was being viewed by the subject at the time of the change of skin conductivity identifies the color related to that particular acupuncture meridian. Using the same method, the color that relates to any other acupuncture meridian can also be identified.

Subjects can benefit more from acupuncture if they are viewing the colors that relate to the meridians in which the needles are placed. Viewing the proper color or colors during terracyclic meditation accompanied by ELF-wave acupuncture will certainly be more beneficial to those who seek to use these methods for stronger Universal Life Field attunement.

Remember, these practices are most effective during the best days of a person's 28-day biorhythm cycle or during the time in the 28-day cycle when it is known that the organ or system in question is super-relating to the Universal Life Field.

Future Subjects

Additional projects must be the subjects of articles in the distant future.

The articles my daughter Deanna and I have in mind for the most immediate future will pertain to the function of the Extraterrestrial Federation, trading houses and lifestyles of some of the most interesting extraterrestrial cultures. We will try to describe some of the unique ET personalities we have dealt with individually over the years. We will also reveal the ultimate reason the extraterrestrials have for observing the progressive demise of the Frequency Barrier.

Castor flex vara gol-vim larpa. Costrina Blac Sace mor mar rit trover. [Author's note: Certain people are involved with the trading houses of Creator and have a particular time in the course of their lives when they would normally come in contact with extraterrestrials. The phrases in this language, Soltec Mal, could activate the dormant telepathic powers of those trained before incarnation in telepathic communication.

20
Introduction To The Federation

by Deanna Bateman

As far back as my earliest memories I have been aware that the lives of my parents and my own were intertwined with the activities of extraterrestrials who were visiting the Earth in spacecraft that the general public referred to as UFOs or flying saucers. I did not find it difficult to keep this awareness to myself and therefore function in the world as any other person of my generation.

For about 30 years (almost on a daily basis) I would be present as my mother carried on conversations with the extraterrestrials by way of my father's telepathic ability. In the earliest days many of the conversations were over my head, but as I reached my teens I was included in the conversations, finding that I could recall with total understanding what had been discussed many years before.

I must say that living with people who carry on daily business (telepathically) with extraterrestrials produces a state of reality that few can easily understand who have not had the experience. The relationship was so strong and real (as it is today) that I have to catch myself from saying something that to me is common knowledge to someone who does not share the belief that extraterrestrials exist, let alone is able to physically contact or telepathically communicate with them. Because there are few who (currently) share my references about the extraterrestrials and their way of life, I tend to find more comfort in and compatibility with the extraterrestrial reality. One might say I am a person (possibly one of many) who functions in this world with a personality influenced during development by input acquired from numerous extraterrestrial sources.

I found the extraterrestrials to be loving and very much like family. I came to call some individuals by the titles "uncle" and "aunt." Even though at times the telepathic conversations were of a serious nature, humor would come through. Even the most lofty-sounding "Lord Copy" might break a slight smile, wink, or make me feel important by asking me what I thought about what was being said.

A great deal of the teachings we received from extraterrestrials was mixed in with stories of our past lives. This method was quite appropriate, as it helped us to retain the information. In most cases it was as if we had always known the information, but were just being refreshed or brought back into mental focus with it. Many people, after hearing the information for the first time, also feel they have always known it. Because I have lived so close to extraterrestrial telepathic communication and its personal influences, I do on occasion find myself coloring my extraterrestrial knowledge with past-life stories. Because things become disjointed in a limited, singular article such as this, an attempt to pass on any important substance and have it comprehended must omit what I feel is the information's spiritually rich and romantic background. Therefore, I know my task is to present the extraterrestrial information I have learned in a basic, objective form.

There are many questions that are asked about the "Federation," such as (1) How old is it? (2) Where was it formed? (3) Who formed it? (4) How was it formed? (5) How wide is its influence? (6) What maintains its solidarity?

The Federation of Worlds is a very ancient organization, having been founded more than 10,000,000 Earth years ago, on Nodia, the third planet of the double star we of Earth call Polaris. The length of time the Federation has been in existence is short compared to the 9-billion-year age of the universe. Prior to the formation of the Federation, human, plant and animal life was abundant throughout the universe. Pre-Federation people, long before space travel was invented, knew of life on other worlds mainly due to some individuals' ability to haphazardly communicate telepathically from one world to another. Because one type of telepathy, called "copy and cancel telepathy," is more easily performed over shorter distances, most of this type of communication took place among people on worlds that are in the same solar system.

Pre-Federation telepathic interaction encouraged space travel to be developed on many planets located in widely separated galaxies throughout the universe. Who achieved space travel first is still unknown. But the question of who came up with the best type of spacecraft for that time is known: it was the Nodians.

The saucer-shaped craft of the Nodians traveled and physically contacted what to them were alien human cultures located on the 11 additional planets of the Polaris system. The Nodians called the double star we call Polaris, Alperlain and Alpercox. The names the other peoples of the solar system call this double star are too numerous to list. I will continue to call this solar system the Polaris system.

Physical contact between the Nodians and the various cultures of the Polaris system was disastrous from the start. No one seemed to have the same religions or morals. Some had greater, and others lesser, psychic abilities than the Nodians. Some races were timid and benevolent and others quite brutish. These cultures were at first restrained within their solar system, but after being transported about in the Nodian spacecraft, began to intermarry and as a byproduct, a society with a "me-first" lifestyle followed. No rules of any particular government or even a creed prevailed. People came and left, taking with them whatever they could barter or steal. Cities on various worlds fell into disrepair and any education that was available was dear. No words can really describe the moral depths to which the people of the Polaris system sank.

When interstellar and intergalactic space travel came into reality, it was found that nearly every other place where space travel had been achieved had also experienced the same ill effects by mixing the cultures of their solar system—even the solar system that contains the planet Earth.

An elite Nodian class (those who controlled the construction and operation of spacecraft) functioned within the chaos. These wealthy trade barons evolved into highly competitive warlords. Working from within their individual organizations, they began to assemble military forces to exert their will. Some of the barons maintained friendly affiliations with others of their kind. With the thought of giving their children an education, several of the barons sent them to be taught by a wise and gentle sage known as Lincore. Lincore's classes were attended not only by the children of the barons, but also by children especially chosen by Lincore.

As time moved forward, three of Lincore's students, by inheritance and self-achievement, came into control of the three most powerful trade houses on the planet Nodia. Though they had been friends as youngsters, they were now competitive to the point of viciousness. To make matters worse, each had acquired the technology of interstellar travel. Each made every effort to bring the worlds of the Polaris system and those of other solar systems into their own particular power base. Interplanetary wars were conducted by surrogates outside the Polaris system. Each baron blamed the others for these distant happenings. It was then that their teacher Lincore stepped in.

Lincore proposed to the three barons that a neutral police force be formed called the "Federation," which would safeguard and protect each of their interests. He got them to agree on the formation of the Federation by promising that each would have successive personal control of the Federation for one Nodian year (about 26 Earth months). The deal was struck that every time one of the trade houses manufactured something that could be considered threatening by the other houses, two of the same items (such as a spacecraft) must be given to the Federation as a buffer. The barons left the Federation's organization to their teacher, Lincore.

Magicians (called skates) and mystics were part of the everyday life of the Nodians – and of every other world, for that matter. Attempts to form religions that worshiped everything from animals to the trade barons never got anywhere. Two types of religious pursuit did not seem to produce spiritual feelings in the peoples of the universe. The first type of religion was based on the worship of the "El." An El is the Master, or nature spirit, of the world. The people found that worshiping the El of their home world with magical rituals would, in some cases, be rewarded with greater magical power. Societies of *macro* magicians were formed wherein the hierarchy was set by the number of tattooed rings that had manifested naturally on the fingers of the magician. Thus the origination of the term "Lord of the Rings." Those able to see auras found that magicians who were "ringed" by their Lord God El possessed a shell of golden light in their psychic aura.

The second form of religion stemmed from the worship of the Els. Practitioners of El worship (due to strange experiences) came to realize that beyond the *macro* level (dimension of the Universal Life Field) of the Els there existed the consciousness of the Supreme Creator. Eventually, after centuries of worshiping the Supreme Creator (still prior to the foundation of the Federation), remarkable individuals began to appear throughout the universe. These individuals, through perseverance and spiritual dedication, had successfully reached the highest form of extrasensory perception and therefore joined their personal consciousness to that of the Supreme Creator. These reperfected beings (sometimes referred to as Angels) and their ability to receive "Lights of Divine Direction" were all part of Lincore's scheme for forming the Federation.

The desire to seek and develop powers that could be used to control others also became a religion based on self-aggrandizement. Those who practiced this way of life came to be called those of the "Other Side of the Wheel."

Both the Federation and the trading houses have established ranks of people known as Lord Copies. These Lord Copies make decisions for the Federation or for the trading houses in which they are employed. The exact function of the Lord Copies will be explained in detail in future articles titled "Federation and the Trade Houses" and "How the Trade Houses Function." When the Lord Copy of any trading house is unable to make a decision about a matter that might affect the spiritual well-being of any people involved, he or she refers the matter to a Lord Copy counterpart of the Federation. If the Lord Copy of the Federation is unable in good conscience to make a decision on the matter, a Light of Divine Direction is requested of one of those that has attained reperfection. These Lights are not always favorable to the trading houses, but are now instantly obeyed, even if doing so means the ruin of a project or even death for the project's participants. With the initiation of the Lights of Divine Direction into the operating procedures of the trading houses and the Federation, Lincore's divinely directed plan was installed to take into consideration the will and purposes of God the Creator.

The influence of the Federation now extends over 298 billion galaxies, or about one-third of the known universe that is reachable by

Federation, or trading house, spacecraft. This area of influence might be viewed in the following way as well: A galaxy can contain anywhere from 5 to 100 million stars (suns), and each sun centers a solar system consisting of 6 to 12 planets; furthermore, each planet existing outside Earth's solar system teems with human life. (We are an exception due to the fact that our fifth planet, Maldek, exploded in the distant past and upset the living environment on most of the other planets, creating the Frequency Barrier on Earth.) Not all planets within the range of Federation influence belong to the Federation. More will be said on this in future articles.

The Federation maintains solidarity in several ways: (1) It controls the numerous trading houses (now existing in numbers too lengthy to record here) by Lights of Divine Direction. (2) It is a repository, evaluator and source of all information pertaining to the physical sciences, medicine and history of all planets with which it has made contact. The names of the two largest repositories for universal knowledge, which are located on Nodia, translate into English as the Cultra-Plat and the Medi-Plat. (3) The Federation employs the universal language, Soltec-Mal, which is the language of the mind and psyche of every human resident of the universe. (4) Universal psychic energy, spent by human emotion and during any act of human creation, is the basis of the Federation's economic system. (5) The Federation does not force any planet to join, nor does it interfere with any member's religion or cultural development – ("the prime directive"). (6) The Federation will come to the physical defense of any planet member as long as Lights of Divine Direction declare that the people of the planet in peril are attempting in good faith to follow as closely as possible the Master Plan of the Supreme Creator.

The Federation has defended this planet and many other worlds from the evil doings of those they call the Other Side of the Wheel. They promise to do so now as well as after the end of the Frequency Barrier. Based on this promise, I feel that we can all sleep safely in our beds tonight.

21

The Trading Houses: This For That

By Deanna Bateman

In the previous chapter, I touched on the formation of the extraterrestrial "Trade Houses" and their relationship to the "Federation." In this chapter I will deal with the development of the now countless number of Trade Houses and their present ways of operation.

Since the formation of the Federation more than ten million years ago, the original three Nodia-based Trading Houses have accumulated material wealth far beyond anyone's ability to imagine. Even those who direct these vast trading empires have no idea how wealthy their particular institution is and don't really care.

The original three Nodian Trading Houses still stand out in the crown of trillions upon trillions of Federation-affiliated Trading Houses that have come into being since the Federation's inception. These later-formed organizations were very important in securing the perpetual existence of the Federation. The original three Trading Houses agreed to submit to the authority of Lincore's Federation for two reasons: to keep peace between themselves and to gain the exclusive use of the Federation's utilities and fire power every third Nodian year (approximately 78 Earth months). In regard to the second reason, it is now known that in the backs of the minds of each of the Trade Barons was this thought: if things were not going the way they personally wanted them to go, they only had to wait until it was their time to control Federation and then wipe out the competition. This sort of action was never taken, again for two reasons: 1. The greedy Barons watched the growing Federation gaining more and more physical power. This was like a carrot on a stick in front of a donkey. In other words, when and if either wanted to make such a move, the Federation would only be stronger at the time they decided to do so. 2. The fact that other Trading Houses were being formed which also contributed two items of strategic value to the Federation for every one of the same item they kept for themselves also changed the picture. The Trading Houses that were formed after the original three established their bases of operation throughout the universe. Therefore, they were not always in the immediate range of the Nodian Group and their attitudes of control. These newcomers were also given the right to use the utilities of Federation once every third Nodian year. This meant that every time one of the three original Trading Houses had the use of the Federation's utilities, they were sharing that same privilege with one third of all the other existing Trading Houses in operation at the time, within the ever expanding boundaries of the Federation. Over the many years that have passed, all the Trading Houses of the Federation, including the original three, came to exist in a state of complete cooperation with each other under the protection and assistance of the "Federation of World."

The English translations for the names of the three original Nodian Trade Houses are Créator, Vonnor and Domfrey.

The Symbols

The general symbol of the Federation is a silver equilateral triangle on a black field. Military units are identified by a solid black equilateral triangle outlined in silver on variously colored backgrounds. The difference in colored backgrounds relates to the psychic color (El Color) of the troops in the unit. There also exists an elite corps of Federation military called "Neuts" (short for Neutrals). A Neut is a man or woman whose soulmate has had "Infinite Thought," and therefore possesses a ring of grey-colored energy in his/her aura. Sometimes Neuts are called Greys, and their symbol is a grey equilateral triangle outlined in silver on a black background. The Neuts are the Federation trouble-shooters. They pick up the pieces whenever anything goes wrong. They fill in as temporary administrators until things are back to normal.

Any kind of military unit might have an additional symbol inside the symbol of the triangle. These sub-symbols are usually symbols of Soltec Mal, the language of the mind. Because the Federation triangle is known universally the three original Trading Houses also adopted individual versions of it. This was originally done to show their relationship to the Federation.

The triangle symbol of the Trading House of Créator has two left sides. The symbol for Créator commerce is a feather quill. The symbolic meaning of the quill is that of the legendary Phoenix Bird, symbol of eternal rebirth. Any promise (deal) signed with this quill means "Once a promise, always a promise."

The symbol for the Créator military is a snake wrapped around a burned-out torch. The symbolic meaning is the defense of the torch of freedom. The burned-out torch indicates that the defense will occur even where freedom is denied.

The triangle symbol of the Trading House of Vonnor has two right sides. The symbol for Vonnor commerce is three stalks of grain. The military symbol of Vonnor is a fiery comet. The predictable orbit of a comet symbolically represents a sentry vigilantly on the lookout and quick to act.

The triangle symbol of the Trading House of Domfrey has two bottom sides. The symbol for Domfrey commerce is the universal symbol for plenty, the cornucopia. The military symbol of Domfrey is a white "X" that symbolically represents the intersection of forces.

Colored backgrounds or outlines for all the symbols are numerous, as they are employed to salute the specific psychic color of the world from which the operator of the spacecraft originated.

Spacecraft of the Federation or any Trade House operating in the skies of Earth are mostly unmarked. Those that are marked usually use the symbol of the feathered serpent, a man with a broken arm or a triangle with three individual lower bars. The symbol is usually red or sky blue in color.

Prior to the time the planet Maldek exploded and the frequency of the explosion caused great geological changes on Mars, leaving the planet in a state of uninhabitability, most native Martians lived inside our solar system. Even so, small groups do maintain livable areas, both under the Martian surface and on the planet's artificial moon, Phobus. On occasion, Martian spacecraft might be seen assisting the Federation conduct Frequency Barrier studies. These craft are marked with the symbol of a large mountain backed by crossed lightning bolts. The mountain in this logo represents the Martian volcano we of Earth call Olympus Mons or Nix Olympus. This volcano covers an area on Mars equal in size to the state of Missouri. The people of the planet Mars do belong to the Federation but long ago they severed their trading ties with the House of Vonnor. They currently have no Trading House affiliations.

Structure of the Trading Houses

Any self-sustaining world that produces a surplus of something of value to someone elsewhere in the Federation can, if they wish, become affiliated with a Trading House. A Trading House can assist a world to become self-sustaining prior to a formal agreement only if this activity has been sanctioned by a favorable Light of Divine Direction. Many worlds do not have governments, and the people live in tribes or clans. These worlds can be contacted only by the Federation and not by a Trading House. The Federation therefore insures the integrity of the Prime Directive (non-interference with the social, technological or spiritual development of a particular planet's inhabitants). Whenever the people of a planet develop a society that operates for the mutual well-being of all, they can become part of the Federation and choose a Trading House affiliation if they want to.

The people of a particular planet, after reaching a point in social development where they can become a member of the Federation, might have only one Trading House available to deal with. The reason for this is that no other Trading House has the knowledge or ability to get to their location in the universe. The Federation does not explore, but the Trading Houses do. If, in the course of Trading House exploration, a world is found that can stand on its own and can live with the shock of extremely advanced technology, it is contacted by an emissary of the Trading House that first discovered its existence. In some cases, worlds are found that are quite advanced but just falling a little short of having a technology equal to that of the Federation or a Trading House. The location of a new area of possible trade is held secret by the Trading House that discovered it. This information is shared only with the Federation. If, by some means, another Trading House shows up on the scene and there is more than one prospect for trade, the

Federation divides the prospects like Solomon.

The extraterrestrials can traverse the vast distances that exist between galaxies. They do this by means of a unique spacecraft propulsion system that requires the craft to position itself in a weak point in the fabric of space (a stargate). Once the propulsion system is activated, the craft is rapidly transported to a specific spot in the universe. The knowledge of the location of stargates and the duration of time the propulsion system should be operated in order to get to a particular point in space is generally kept secret from all other Trading Houses by the Trading House that originally gained the knowledge. This is to protect any interests they are developing. Eventually the stargate information is shared with other Trading Houses, but most of the time it is sold to them. For more information pertaining to exraterrestrial spacecraft propulsion, see my father's book, *Dragons and Chariots*.

The Trading Houses act as brokers for goods. Their expertise in knowing who wants or needs something and who has it is their key to commercial success. The ability to pick up and deliver goods or products over great stellar distances or to trade for things they themselves have produced also makes their activities profitable for all concerned. It was explained in an earlier article that psychic energy (charge force) backs the economic system of the extraterrestrial Federation. The Trading Houses work within this system and thus find that taking a profit hurts nobody.

One time an official of an extraterrestrial Trading House said, "In the earliest of days it came about that we realized that we were trading dogs for dog food, to get more dogs to get more dog food. We were saved from this endless escalation when Federation decreed that living animals could not be moved from one planet to another without the permission of a favorable Light of Divine Direction. At times things like this are bound to happen, especially when one makes a living exchanging this for that."

My next article will be about what it means to a Trading House to have the use of Federation facilities and how the Trading Houses function.

22

The Trading Houses: Part 2

By Wesley and Deanna Bateman

When permitted by a favorable Light of Divine Direction to form a trading relationship with a new member of the Federation (see Part 1 in the April issue), a Trading House sends teams of highly paid experts to that world to gather as much information about it as possible. The method of gathering and storing this information is unique. For example, an expert in biology will study everything about the world's biological makeup from the position of his or her prior knowledge and perspective. The expert's opinions, as educated observations, are mentally recorded on a material substance that is sensitive to the bioelectrical thoughts of the expert.

The ROM

This pill-sized recording is called a "Rhom." With the development of computer technology on the Earth, our original spelling, Rhom, was changed to correlate with current computer jargon: ROM (Read Only Memory). The copies of the ROMs of the experts of every field are dispatched to the Federation and the central Trading House headquarters. They will be used later if it becomes necessary to provide superior guidance in any case in which a situation arises in the world that cannot be settled satisfactorily in a physical and/or amiable spiritual manner by local Trading House representatives.

The ROMs are used as if they were the actual memory of the person who is attempting to resolve the problem. These important, high-ranking decision-makers of the Trading Houses are called Lord Copies. A Lord Copy might have never visited the world in question, but on mental activation of the planet's ROM bank, everything that the original ROM-making experts saw and evaluated becomes integrated into the actual memory of the Lord Copy. Therefore, the Lord Copy has all the expert references and opinions from which to draw to formulate a decision about action. If a Lord Copy cannot form a decision, the matter is passed on to a Lord Copy of higher station.

There are an endless number of telepathic frequencies, each related exclusively to a place in the microlevel of the Universal Life Field. A telepath who can communicate on all levels of the microlevel is called a Zero Copy. To qualify as a Lord Copy a person must have Zero Copy ability. Individual telepaths are limited to operating only on certain planes of the microlevel. For example, a Copy Five can telepathically communicate on every mental frequency above five, but not on mental frequencies zero through four. As a second example, a Copy Six can telepathically communicate on all telepathic frequencies above six, but cannot communicate on telepathic mental frequencies of zero through five.

If no Lord Copy of a Trading House is able to make a decision or one does form a course of action that will work but might affect the life or the spiritual progress of anyone involved, the course of action under consideration is mentally related to a Lord Copy of the Federation. If the Lord Copy of the Federation agrees with the course of action proposed by the Trading House lord, the action is permitted. If the Federation Lord Copy cannot in good conscience agree with the plan of action, a Light of Divine Direction is requested. A white light indicates that the plan will not interfere with anyone or anything that is trying to progress within the master plan of the most supreme Creator. A black light (actually no light) means the direct opposite. A grey light indicates that the results of the action will only stall things and the cause of the problem will some day come back to haunt those involved.

Educational Fun

ROMs are also used by the extraterrestrials for entertainment and education. They are very useful for these purposes because their contents can be physically and emotionally experienced in a compressed time frame. To explain this, let us refer to the experiences of people who are facing immediate danger of losing their lives and how they relate that their entire lives flashed before their minds' eyes. This phenomenon occurs when the endangered person involuntarily accelerates the memory process, scanning the memory contents of the brain for any physical experience or knowledge that could be now employed to get him or her out of the dire situation.

As an audio or video tape can be played back by appropriate machinery, a ROM can be played back by a human brain. While this is being done, the person engaged in the playback will experience each and every physical feeling and emotion that was being experienced by the person who made the ROM. If the ROM-maker had been watching a fireworks display on a balmy summer evening, the person experiencing the ROM's contents will mentally stand in for the ROM-maker and feel the summer breeze, hear and see the fireworks display, and smell the burned gunpowder. If the ROM-maker had an itch and scratched it with a stick, the ROM-reader will experience doing the same.

Reading a ROM

The ROM-reader loses identity and assumes the identity of the ROM-maker, experiencing the events and sensations as if they were happening for the first time. Climbing dangerous mountains, racing at high speed, or viewing the landscape of a distant world are actions available on ROMs for experiencing personally. Because the mental scan rate can be accelerated, experience that took the ROM-maker years to record can be compressed into minutes during mental playback. During the playback, the ROM-reader actually spends the years eating, sleeping, dreaming, working and loving as the original ROM-maker might have done many thousands of years ago. It is often said that "life is an illusion." Maybe you are now on a distant world where you began reading a ROM several minutes ago. That ROM is a record of the life of a person who once lived on the Planet Earth millions of years ago.

In some cases, every world existing in an individual solar system is affiliated by trade with one particular Trading House. Each world has a representative of that Trading House living on it. Whenever it becomes possible, any "off-worlders" who might have administered trading affairs at the beginning of the affiliation are replaced by natives.

Most Trading Houses maintain a defensive military presence in a solar system in which they have interests. The chief of such forces, if in command of forces that protect one solar system, wears one star as a symbol of rank. If his or her authority extends to two solar systems, two stars are worn as a symbol of rank. Is it not curious that most military organizations on the Earth use the star as the symbol for the rank of general? The Federation also maintains a defensive military presence, not solar system by solar system, but galaxy by galaxy. If the forces of the Federation are required to assist those of a Trading House in any conflict, they are dispatched only if permitted to do so by a Light of Divine Direction. Upon arrival the Federation forces fall under command of the highest ranking commander, even if this commander is an officer of the Trading House.

All Trading House officers were trained and originally commissioned by the Federation. Trading Houses can reward and elevate one of their military officers in any way except by raising them in rank. Only the Federation can raise such an officer in rank.

Use of the Federation's Utilities

Every third Nodian year, one-third of the Federation Trading Houses have the use of the nonmilitary utilities of the Federation. An example of this usage is as follows: If three spacecraft from three separate Trading Houses require that they be picked up and transported by a Federation mothership and there is room for only one craft, the craft belonging to the Trading House "having Federation" gets the ride, because one or the other of the original Nodian Trading Houses along with one-third of the Federation's other Trading Houses have Federation at the same time. For simplicity, the one-Nodian-year periods of Federation usage are called the Créator, Vonnor, and Domfrey periods. Federation will not transport a Trading House spacecraft to any place that the Trading House does not have a trade interest. However, they do not prevent a Trading House from going to an area that is exclusive to another Trading House; therefore, the giant Trading Houses of Créator, Vonnor and Domfrey have built their own galaxy-traveling motherships at the price of giving the Federation two for each one.

Some (but not all) galactic motherships of the Trading Houses and Federation are so large they cannot orbit a planet without causing the planet's ocean tides to rise dangerously or the planet's orbit around its sun to become unstable. These motherships are usually stationed outside of the solar lens (solar system). A mothership that does come into a solar system does not take up an orbit around a planet, but instead allows the gravitational forces of the system's sun to slowly pull it toward the center of the system like a comet. When the mothership gets too far into the system it powers up and returns to the solar system's outer boundaries, there to resume the process of being drawn back toward the system's center by the sun.

Life on a Mothership

Federation and Trading House motherships are immense, some ranging up to 450 miles in diameter and 100 miles high. These vehicles, which are capable of inter-galactic travel, were constructed in space over thousands of years. This type of craft exists in incomprehensible numbers. Parts for them come from worlds far and wide. The Trading House mothercraft spend considerable time transporting commercial cargoes, while most of the Federation mothercraft do the same for the Trading Houses that have the use of their services at the time.

Other than performing cargo transport duties, a mothership is equipped to wage war. On its lowest decks can be found thousands of craft built exclusively for battle. The collective term for this fleet of warships is the litter. In the blink of an eye these craft can be launched into space for the protection of the mothership. While being stored, the circular parabolic reflecting dishes of these craft are removed and stacked on each other as one would stack dishes. This procedure allows technicians to gain easier access to the propulsion system for repairs or maintenance.

Decks above the litter decks are reserved for craft that are being transported for one reason or another. In some cases the operators of these craft do not leave the confines of the craft. This is because the mothership's Rad atmosphere, easily breathed by most people, is not easily breathed by some extraterrestrial races without a period of adaptation. Because the period of Rad adaptation might take longer than the period of transport to their destination, some choose simply to remain sealed aboard their ships, continuing to breathe their own atmospheres.

Most extraterrestrials have the same physiology as we of the Earth have. A few exceptions are some ET races that have two hearts or three to four kidneys. In all cases, every human, no matter his or her physiology, can mate and produce offspring.

All craft, including the mothership's litter, carry their own weight by connecting their individual propulsion systems to the propulsion system of the mothership. A mothership is a world unto itself; some have populations that range in the millions. The operation of the craft is conducted by a considerable number of telepathic copies. Those at the top of the command structure are the only ones who are aware of the location of certain stargates. The locations of stargates are in most cases kept secret by the Federation or by the particular Trading House that originally found them. It is sometimes worth it to block a stargate from a mothership, thus denying its use (no two things can occupy the same space at the same time). Smaller craft equipped for space warp can enter a mothership at speeds up to 10,000 miles per hour. These smaller craft do not stop but instead get a shot of energy from the mothership and instantly enter the stargate. The stargate's center in such a case is located inside the confines of the mothership.

The command center of a mothership is really a spacecraft in its own right. It can be separated from the main body of the vehicle at will. This is done if emissary business is to be conducted in a solar system or if any area of the main body becomes seriously damaged. The occupants of the command center, by Federation Law, cannot separate the command center from the main body or launch the litter without first receiving a favorable Light of Divine Direction.

Cells of the Reborn

At the time of the Federation's founding, some people recalled having lived before. As time went on, more and more people began to recall past lives. Eventually, people who in past lives had been Lord Copies for Trading Houses and the Federation began to re-embody. When reaching maturity some of these reborns were actually better qualified to hold their original position than those who were holding the position at the time. This caused cells of officials directed by the most qualified to be formed. The cells were composed of persons then living who at one time in the present life or in some previous life had held the particular position. Sometimes these reborns become emissaries for Trading Houses or the Federation under terms of a Royal Contract. These Royal Contracts have unlimited economic power. They can singularly speak and deal for the highest director of their organization as a peer.

Rebirth is a reality, and people have the option of passing on part or all of their material possessions to their heirs or to the Federation for safekeeping. Any part of their possessions that is given to the Federation is held in trust and invested by the Federation in Federation projects. Federation investments can be made on any world in the Federation. The wealth that is collectively attained from countless trusts is called the "Wealth of the River." The Wealth of the River is generally used to raise the standard of living of the people of one world or of all the people of the Federation. Upon rebirth the person's past-life possessions and wealth are returned to his or her personal control, with interest. See, you can take it with you!

The Akashic Records

Each and every planet in the universe has a magnetic field that surrounds it. The planetary magnetic fields act like ROM recorders, and record the life experiences of each and every person who ever lived on the planet. These ROM records have come to be named the Akashic Records. From these records sensitives on the Earth and elsewhere can tune in to any past life of an inquiring person. This practice is not needed by the extraterrestrials because they remember every one of their past lives. In fact, they say that each past life blends with the present life as if there were hardly an interruption between them. There are times when a person who is capable of reading Akashic Records can find very few previous lifetimes or no previous lifetime at all for an individual. The reason for this is that the person in question lived only a few lifetimes or no previous lifetime at all on the planet. This is to say that the person might have lived thousands of previous lifetimes on other planets, but the records of those lifetimes can be found only in the Akashic Records of those planets.

Crime

We asked if there was crime in the Federation, and if there was, what was done about it. The reply was that there is crime. Things are considered crimes when they violate the spiritual rights of others. Some things that are considered crimes on the Earth are considered so only to protect the rule of governments or the assets of a chosen few. The Federation does not interfere with or consider a crime any practice, economic or moral, that is not in violation of the Master Plan of the Supreme Creator. Criminals are dealt with in a variety of ways, depending upon in which world the crime was committed. There are as many ways for dealing with criminals as there are worlds in the universe. Some worlds exercise long-standing methods of punishment that were originally imparted to them by their parent El. Most Federation worlds employ a method of criminal restraint called the Screen.

When a person is apprehended for a crime, even one of murder, to take his or her life in return serves nothing, because as time passes, the executed criminal is reborn, exonerated of the crime because the price of it had been determined and carried out. Many who commit a crime of the spirit would welcome death as a payment for their transgressions, knowing that what they got for committing the crime is worth more to them than the cost of retribution. Therefore the criminal is left free to live and work among the general public under the restraints of a brainwave monitoring, transmitting and receiving instrument.

If the person begins to formulate thoughts related to criminal behavior, the instrument receives this information and transmits mental symbols that defeat the criminal's thought processes. The criminal is thus restrained from carrying out any crime. A person can be sentenced to be monitored by the screen for one or more lifetimes. Periodically, the subject can petition for Lights of Divine Direction in the hope that a favorable Light will set him or her free from mental monitoring.

The Institutions

The Federation maintains two institutions that are called, in English, the Cultra-Plat and the Med-Plat. The Cultra-Plat is both a teaching institution and a repository of information that pertains to every facet of a particular culture, past and present, of each world of the Federation. The Med-Plat is also a teaching institution, one that deals with the various forms of medicine that are practiced on every Federation world. The Cultra-Plat also catalogs the various forms of plant and animal life that exist in the Federation. The extraterrestrials tell us that many of the animals of the Earth, even those that are extinct, can be found throughout the universe. In some cases the animals are different in size and physiology. As well, there exist animals in the universe that never walked on the Earth.

Extraterrestrial foods are, in general, synthetics, but there are people of some worlds who eat meat due to the religious instruction of their parent El.

It is not forbidden for an extraterrestrial person from one world to mate with a person of another world, but it is not recommended, based on the emotional and spiritual chaos it can cause for any children that come from such a union. Interplanetary marriage was the ruin of many a culture at the beginning of space travel.

The Antimatter Universe

The extraterrestrials tell us that we live in a positive universe where matter is composed of positively charged protons and neutrons and negatively charged electrons. They also tell us that there exists a universe of antimatter consisting of negatively charged protons and positively charged electrons. The positive universe and the antimatter universe are separated by a river of energy they call the riff. On rare occasions the riff opens, and bodies such as stars and galaxies pass from the antimatter universe into the positive universe. In the process, the antimatter transmutes into positive matter. After any body comes through the riff, it closes behind the body. The dinosaurs of Earth were once antimatter creatures. Their fossil remains are now composed of positive matter.

23
The Christ Reality

by Wesley and Deanna Bateman

A myriad of stars and planets, an infinite interstellar glory of uncharted galaxies and uncounted worlds; these are the miracles of creation we must consider.

Yes, there are miraculous things that exist in the vast universe. Life is a miraculous reality. But where does reality as we know it come from? What about the manifestation of new realities? It may or may not be a surprise to you, the reader, that we as humans have had and still have the power to manifest new realities. In fact, the extraterrestrials are counting on us of the Earth to manifest a new reality, a reality that will lift a psychic burden off many of them, as well as off ourselves.

The development of this "New Reality" is exclusively related to the Earth and its relationship to the Frequency Barrier. The protection of this reality and the encouragement of its manifestation are the ultimate, underlying reasons the extraterrestrials have for visiting the Earth. The extraterrestrials call this forthcoming new addition to the universe "The Christ Reality."

More than two thousand Earth years ago, the extraterrestrials brought a subject of great concern before those who possess the ability to perceive the will of the Supreme Creator. The reason for this concern lay in the fact that it had become evident that many people were being reborn time and time again without making any spiritual progress according to the Master Plan. In all cases, these people were restricted from making spiritual progress by those who had psychically enslaved them lifetime after lifetime, by the means of controlling their personal destiny patterns. The following question was put to those of re-perfection: "Will there ever be a solution that will free the psychically enslaved from their "other-side-of-the-wheel masters, the forces of darkness? The re-perfected ones responded to this concern with Lights of Divine Direction. By the process of elimination, the extraterrestrials eventually learned that the solution to this spiritual dilemma would come in the form of a man, and that man would be born in the Frequency Barrier of the planet Earth.

Jesus was that man. He went from birth to death on the cross, without putting a destiny distortion into his aura. In so doing, he initiated the new reality, now referred to as the Christ Reality.

It is recorded in the *Apocrypha* (the lost books of the Bible), as it is in the present versions of the Bible, that the three wise men followed a star to Bethlehem. But in the *Apocrypha* it says that the star came down from the sky, parked on a mountaintop and waited for the Magi astride their camels to catch up. The Star of Bethlehem was an extraterrestrial spacecraft from which the shepherds received the audible message, "Fear not; for, behold I bring you tidings of great joy, which shall be to all people. For unto you is born this day in the city of David, a Savior, who is Christ the Lord. And this will be a sign unto you; ye shall find the babe wrapped in swaddling cloths lying in a manger." (Luke 2: 10-12.)

The stories about the healing miracles and the teachings of Jesus Christ are well known, but there are some things about the life and purpose of Jesus Christ that become a little clearer in the light of extraterrestrial information. One thing is related to how he spoke to vast multitudes of people and was heard by all. The extraterrestrials tell us that he did indeed speak audibly, but he also spoke telepathically. Each one of the assembly heard him clearly without realizing that they were listening to his words telepathically.

When Jesus came upon a crowd about to stone a woman for the sin of adultery, he bent before several individuals in the crowd and wrote in the dirt, "robber, thief, adulterer and murderer." He then said, "He who is without sin cast the first stone." Jesus had read the auras of the belligerents and saw that they had been guilty of the sins he wrote before them, either in their present life or in a previous lifetime. His spiritual authority rang true and was not questioned by any of the crowd. They freed the woman.

Jesus once found a beggar who was deaf and mute. He bent down, picked up some dirt and spat on it, making mud. He took the mud on his finger tips, placed it into the beggar's ears and looking to the sky cried out the word "Ephphatha." The word ephphatha is a transliteration to Greek of an ancient Aramaic phrase which in English means "Be thou opened." The beggar then regained his hearing and speech.

Many physical problems are caused when certain senses are not being evaluated by the brain. This is similar to a person who, while under hypnosis, is told that he will either not see, feel or taste some specific thing. The receptors in the brain are turned off, disconnected. Jesus brought the man out of a hypnotic state and opened up the receptive sensors of the beggar's brain, thus allowing him to speak and hear again.

From the cross, Jesus said, "Father, forgive them, for they know not what they do." The Frequency Barrier was more intense at that time than it is at the present, and he asked the Supreme Creator to take that fact into consideration and not judge or punish his executioners harshly, or at all.

It is said that during the crucifixion there was a great earthquake. That earthquake was the first one to start the Frequency Barrier of the Earth back onto an unerring course toward its final extinction.

It is evident that Christianity, as well as other faiths, have participated in establishing and maintaining the growth of civilization on the Earth. It has never been the wish of the Federation to violate the Prime Directive relating to noninterference with the religions of a planet and they assure us they are not interfering. The Earth was a Federation member prior to the beginning of the Frequency Barrier, and the religion of Christianity originated on the Earth and was not extraterrestrially inspired. In order to fulfill the Divine purpose of the Christ Reality, the following must be understood, or Christianity will never become that which it was Divinely intended to be: Currently, we have "churchianity" rather than Christianity. We must, of course change this situation.

A new reality such as the Christ Reality must be believed in in order for it to manifest into a permanent universal reality. The problem here is that some people say, "I can't believe in something that is not a reality." Let us repeat: the Christ Reality can manifest only if a psychic energy is given to it by the majority of people on Earth in the form of sincere belief. For the strongest results, this must be accomplished before the Frequency Barrier is gone. The Christ Reality is like a flower in a hot house, the extraterrestrials do not want to disturb its growth in any way. This is why they do not just ignore the Frequency Barrier and wait for it to go away. They are not going to miss any opportunity to bring the wondrous manifestation of the Christ Reality to a fruitful conclusion.

Space is the "bottomless pit" described in the Book of Revelation. The Frequency Barrier keeps both the good and the evil in space from physically living on the Earth. Jesus said, "Where a carcass is, the vultures will gather." This means that when the Frequency Barrier is gone, the forces of darkness will descend upon the planet like vultures. If things come to this, the Federation is prepared to physically repel any such attacks.

In the mean time, the Federation has sent the spiritual essences of many people to embody on the Earth as members of the Patrax, the Divine plan. The ultimate goal of the Patrax is the manifestation of the Christ Reality. It also acts as a deterrent for counter measures that might be initiated *in the same way* by the "Forces of Darkness." Those of the Patrax are sworn to work toward the ultimate goal, and always keep in mind that *what is important is the message and not the messenger.*

Ephphatha

The Ephphatha Group is composed of persons from many occupations and professions who have combined their talents and other personal resources in order to investigate certain unexplained phenomena. The purpose of conducting these studies is to determine whether any data acquired can be used to benefit mankind, especially in the areas of health, energy technology, and most especially, in the areas of spirituality, ecology and world peace.

Ephphatha Group membership will be expanded in the near future. Look for future announcements.

24

Not on Your Life or Mine

I have often been asked why I do not give private channeling sessions. After all, there are many who would pay well to talk to the extraterrestrials. My reply has always been, "My financial future would be rosy, if it were only that easy."

First of all, I am not a channel as channels go, but I am a telepath. Please believe me there is a vast difference.

An authentic channel provides all of the psychic energy and molar-level mental focus for the communication session, whereas most of their contacts are disembodied and cannot provide the faculties. Any disembodied being that communicates to an embodied person (channel) does so to participate in and enjoy the sensations of life, and also to profit by the psychic energy that might be emotionally given by those listening to what they have to say. Any embodied extraterrestrials that would provide personal information for an individual via an Earthly channel would definitely have a highly important reason to do so. Such a reason could be benign or malevolent, only time would tell. You can be sure that such communications would not be directed to each and every person asked for personal communication. The cost in psychic energy would be astronomical, and the life span of the extraterrestrial and the channel would be limited to the amount of psychic energy they could somehow obtain from others.

A malevolent extraterrestrial might not care if the channel's life is depleted as long as their purpose (whatever it is) for communication is on the path to success. Neither type of extraterrestrial will deliberately tell a lie because telling a lie costs the liar irretrievable psychic energy. A malevolent extraterrestrial will usually present telepathic information designed to instill false understanding or cause the receiver to make assumption. In this manner the extraterrestrial transmitter is not viewed as a liar under the rules of the Master Plan. If the telepathic receiver passes any false understanding or assumption on to others as the truth, the original receiver and all who perpetrate the false information thereafter will accordingly lose psychic energy.

First of all, to find an extraterrestrial that was willing to be telepathically at my instant beck and call for the purpose of passing on personal information to some paying customer would not be worth talking to. Such an extraterrestrial would be considered an idiot with suicidal tendencies by his peers. I would be looked upon as idiot number two. The extraterrestrials are aware that telepathic communication is very costly in psychic life force and to trade this valuable energy in the form of telepathic communication for money would be stupid.

There are many things worth the great cost of psychic energy to relate telepathically. These things pertain to the establishment of trust and spiritual bonding. In other words, things that would be beneficial to us of the Earth and to the benign extraterrestrials alike. Such information is communicated once and only once (the time it takes to do is not considered) and generally applies to all the people of the planet.

If we look at the majority of channeled material, we find it to be mostly repetitious, i.e., "There are changes taking place. There are going to be changes taking place. Love one another. Love yourself." I for one have got the message. But where is the rest of the story, such as: How are the extraterrestrials traversing the great distance of space? How do their spacecraft operate? Why have they been visiting the Earth for thousands of years? These are only a few questions one would intelligently ask an extraterrestrial if one had their physical or telepathic attention.

Over the past thirty some years I have asked my extraterrestrial contacts these questions and thousands more. In no case were they reluctant to answer that is, if the answer did not violate the "Prime Directive" (not to interfere with the natural development of our civilization, or any part of our spiritual growth).

My ability to understand the answers the extraterrestrials gave to my questions is another story. To understand a telepathic message to any degree, it is necessary to have as many mental references about the subject as possible. In many cases, I came up short of mental references about a particular subject, and therefore failed to fully comprehend the extraterrestrial answer to my question or a description of a particular subject. Even so, the extraterrestrials encouraged me to seek out more references about the subject, and even directed my efforts to the most appropriate data sources that were within my ability to acquire. Gradually, I was able to fully understand or at least come to a greater understanding of what the extraterrestrial telepaths on the other end were saying. In many cases, the extraterrestrials manipulated mental references in a manner that can only be described as mental acrobatics. Months, and sometimes years, might have passed before something said by a friend, or something read in a book might cause all previously opened-ended references about a subject to gel, and therefore finally make sense.

While thinking of the many ways and means the extraterrestrials employed to answer my questions I am reminded of a short poem by William Blake:

To see a world in a grain of sand.
And a heaven in a flower,
Hold infinity in the palm of your hand,
And eternity in an hour.

In so many cases of telepathy, it depends how one looks at things.

No channel or telepath is worth a farthing unless the information they are receiving and imparting has practical educational worth. Telepathy is a natural ability in the frequency barrier-free "Open State." Within a matter of years this ability will also be commonplace among all persons living on the Earth (after the frequency barrier has disappeared). Hopefully, we will have the direct physical guidance of benign extraterrestrials to bring us through the initial stages of confusion and help us to handle and use this newly awakening mental ability (as well as other psi abilities).

For the time being, be content to allow things to unfold naturally; not everyone need be a channel or telepath. It is a way of life some might not find to be very romantic. Remember it's the "message, not the messenger" that is important. You might do great things with the messages that are far beyond the understanding or ability of the channel or telepath that brought the information into this realm of reality.

What's Really Going On?

The UFO mystery has been long solved. The fact that occupants of extraterrestrial spacecraft (so-called UFOs) have been observing frequency barrier-related earthquakes and volcanic eruptions for thousands of years and more recently nuclear bomb detonations has been known by the U.S. and other governments of the world for more than 50 years. Some foreign governments (Brazil, for one) have openly stated that they know for certain that some UFOs are extraterrestrial spaceships.

The question is often asked: "Why doesn't the government tell the public the truth about extraterrestrial visitations to the Earth?"

After various interactions with government agents (occurring almost 30 years ago) the bottom-line reason for not telling the public the truth about UFOs was: "The truth will disrupt the function of the two most important factors that hold our civilization together – the economy and religion." Some day we will have to accept these pending disruptions and their aftermath. But because the extraterrestrials cannot say for sure when the frequency barrier will be gone, we must maintain things as they are for the good of the planet. In the meantime, the extraterrestrials will continue to conduct their business as usual; after all, we are not capable of opposing them militarily, nor do we want to. At the present time we can publicly state that the UFOs are no apparent threat to the security of the United States, or of any other country, for that matter.

The Federation of Worlds has informed us of their agenda; it is designed to produce as little disruption to our Earthly activities as possible. Where and when the extraterrestrial activities do cause public alarm, we will do our best to play the occurrence down and will absorb any criticism or challenges the minority of believers might make against our credibility. Our goal is to produce more skeptics than UFO believers among the world's populations. Sometimes we win a few, sometimes we lose a few, so the mystery continues in the public mind. What the public does not know about the UFOs won't hurt them. It is our sincere opinion that public knowledge that pertains to the fact that extraterrestrials from throughout the universe have been visiting the Earth will cause a definite degree of disorder and possible anarchy and chaos.

The fact that the government is aware of the existence of the frequency barrier was mentioned in a previous section of this writing in the form of a quote from a United States Air Force Academy text book: "Extraterrestrials might have tried to contact us on a different plane of awareness and we are not yet sensitive to such a plane." The statement, "We are not yest sensitive to such a plane" does reveal that the government knows about the existence of the frequency barrier and believes the extraterrestrials when they say that when the barrier disappears we will be able to communicate easily with them (telepathically) on a different, higher plane of awareness.

Over the years the governments of the Earth have come to accept the fact that the extraterrestrials are communicating telepathically with some individuals on the Earth. It has been the government's policy to make anyone publicly relating true extraterrestrial information look like a fool, a crackpot. If this ploy doesn't work, then an attempt is made to discredit the person by falsely accusing them of such things as child molestation, operating a prostitution ring or selling illegal drugs. They also threaten to falsely accuse and arrest persons for crimes they did not commit, unless they refrain from publicly relating UFO information that originated from a true extraterrestrial source. I personally, have been threatened in this manner. The government's final solution is to cause the death of the person or persons relating true extraterrestrial information. These deaths alway appear to be the result of suicide or some type of fatal accident.

In September of 1991, I returned from Sedona, Arizona, to my home in Rimrock, Arizona (about 30 miles apart), and decided to take a bath. Pulling back the shower curtain I found a deadly coral snake coiled on the bottom of the tub. I destroyed the creature with a shovel. Within a few days, my daughter, Deanna, was airlifted to Phoenix, Arizona, with a mysterious illness. She hovered near death for months before the doctors realized that she had ingested something that had killed off intestinal bacteria and if left unopposed will produce very poisonous toxins. This type of illness is almost always fatal. She recovered from that ordeal but is not in perfect health. I have no doubt in my mind that my public return to the UFO field after thirty years of silence has angered some government agency who wishes me silenced forever.

Proof of Extraterrestrial Existence and Contact

The extraterrestrials wish to impart the fact that the explosion (destruction) of the planet Maldec caused most of the planets of our solar system to become uninhabitable. They state that the area known as Cydonia on Mars represents proof that humans once lived on that planet more than 500,000 years ago.

They also want us to know that the frequency barrier exists, and that they have been watching it diminish for thousands of years by observing related earthquakes, volcanic erruptions and more recently, nuclear bomb detonations.

The extraterrestrials want us to understand the importance, and the value of the "charge force" (psychic energy).

The benign extraterrestrials also want us to know that there are those (both on and off the Earth) who do not have our best interests at heart. They also want us to know how to recognize, avoid and counter those with such malevolent motives.

For the most part, extraterrestrials want us to help in the manifestation of the Christ Reality. Whereas, this reality will spiritually benefit all mankind, both on the Earth and on each and every inhabited planet in the universe.

The extraterrestrials have given us a number of "Patrax Projects" that they feel would be of help to us and would not violate the Prime Directive. They are listed without a description of their subject matter. A detailed description of each and every project and stage of development will become avilable in the near future. The names of thes projects are: Ephphatha, Prism, Fountain, Eden, Drago, Chariot, Blessingstone, Midas, Valhalla, Crown and Circle.

The extraterrestrials have give us the secret of their spacecraft propulsion systems, and as well, the methods they ust to rapidly traverse the vast distances of space. This information can be found in by book *Dragons and Chariots*.

The fact that extraterrestrials have visited Earth in the distant paxst is proven beyond all doubt by my three volume series: *The Rods of Amon Ra*. This work is the result of more than 20 years of constant telepathic contact with extraterrestrials. This series describes the natural system of mathematics which is now know as the Ra System, and how this system was employed in the construction of the Great Pyramid of Giza, the second and third pyrimids of Giza, and other ancient sites such as Stonehenge (England), Tiahuanaco (Bolivia), Teotihuacan (Mexico), Palenque (Mexico) and Cydonia (planet Mars). For more mathmatical data on Cydonia, see Michael Lee's book, *Cydonia Decoded.*

At the time of this writing, a fourth volume of the *Rods of Amon Ra* is being authored by Randolph W. Masters and myself. It is titled *Drums of Ice, Harps of Fire: An Explanation of Ramathized Music Based On the Geometry of the Great Pyramid.*

The Ra System has allowed us to isolate the duration of the Natural Second of Time and also to identify the frequencies of musical notes that are compatable to human brainwave frequencies. Recorded Ra Music will also be available in the near future.

As time goes on, new volumes of the *Rods of Amon* will become available as the relationship of the Ra System to physics, chemistry, medicine, and so on, are firmly established. Those who have references in these fields (professional or not) are being sought to review their knowledge in light of the Ra System of Mathematics.

Be of good cheer – the wonderful adventure of life goes on.